Alexis

MY TRUE STORY
of Being Seduced by
an Online Predator

by **Alexis Singer** edited by Deborah Reber

HCI
TEENS

Health Communications, Inc.
Deerfield Beach, Florida

www.hcibooks.com

Library of Congress Cataloging-in-Publication Data

Singer, Alexis, 1990-
    Alexis : my true story of being seduced by an online predator / by
Alexis Singer.
      p. cm.
   ISBN-13: 978-0-7573-1529-9
   ISBN-10: 0-7573-1529-1
   1. Singer, Alexis—Sexual behavior.   2. Computer sex—United States.
3. Teenage girls—Sexual behavior—United States—Biography.   I. Title.
HQ27.5.S56 2010
306.7092—dc22
[B]

                                              2010016988

©2010 Health Communications, Inc.

Publisher: Health Communications, Inc.
               3201 S.W. 15th Street
               Deerfield Beach, FL 33442–8190

Cover design by Larissa Hise Henoch
Interior formatting by Dawn Von Strolley Grove

For my mother, my friends, and my boyfriend,
Colin, for being there for me through
everything, even the writing of this
book. And for all of the other kids
who've gone through something
similar to this, keep holding steady.

Chapter I

I WISH I HAD KNOWN THE FUTURE when an instant message (IM) popped up in the top right corner of my laptop screen on June 29, 2007. In that moment, I wish I had been able to foresee all the consequences of one minor exchange and closed down that window. If I could go back now and see that message and predict the two and a half years of trauma it would cause, the relationships it would ruin, and the lives it would change, I would have ignored it, shut off my computer, and cracked open a book. Maybe I would have doused my seventeen-inch PowerBook with lighter fluid and set it ablaze. If I had known what would happen because of one seemingly inconsequential conversation, I would have quit the Internet for good, forgotten technology existed, and started writing all of my papers on stone tablets by candlelight.

But on June 29, 2007, I didn't close my computer when a little six-word message popped up in the corner of my screen. I was in no position to ignore human contact, no matter how distant and shady it was. I was fresh off my junior year of high school, by far the most stressful year of my life. All of the friends I'd had for years had outgrown me, leaving me to flail helplessly in the already choppy sea of high school. I had broken up with my first and only boyfriend six months earlier, ending an on-and-off relationship that had lasted over three years, and I had been hopelessly single ever since. All in all, I had suffered through the last six months trying to balance the SAT, the never-easy process of making new friends, AP courses, a father who was divorcing my stepmother, and a part-time job that I dreaded even more than everything else in my life. And through it all, I found myself sitting on my bed every night staring at my computer screen, riding the waves of each daily crisis completely and totally alone.

That may have been an attitude rather than a circumstance, but in high school we're all loners, at least from our own perspectives. That's the way it works. I didn't have a single friend in high school who didn't spend several hours a day with their eyes glued to a monitor. It's escapism in its most luring form, especially for people who have a hard time being themselves in person. We all find our niche. For me, it was a message board I discovered my sophomore year—a section of a theater message board pushed off to the side for those of us who wanted to talk about real life, politics, and entertainment. Despite some harassment from a particularly mean and sarcastic user (every message board has at least one), I fell in pretty quickly there. In no time I made a few "friends," in the loose way you can call people you've never seen face-to-face and whose last names you do not know, friends. I found a rhythm there. It was a place to go and escape the difficulty of everyday life. When I didn't feel like talking to my parents about my English essay on *Death of a Salesman*, I could go onto The Board (as it became known in my head) and talk about how badly I thought George W. Bush was screwing up or how last week's episode of *The Office* wasn't as funny as the rest of the season. And there were even people there who cared about what I had to say from time to time. No matter what kind of day I was having, I could usually count on someone posting an approving response to my hilarious comment about Britney Spears.

I had found The Board the previous summer while spending most of my days barricaded in my room. My father, who got married in 2004 and split with his now-ex-wife in late 2005, was unavailable most of the time and my friends, the few who hadn't stopped liking me in the past year, were off doing fun things with their families or each other and leaving me out. So, I sat in my room and surfed the Web. At the time I was into theater and stumbled onto prominent websites that covered the theater world. When I found The Board, I attached myself to it like a parasite, trying my best to fit in with the ragtag users of the site and making fast friends with several of the regulars, exchanging occasional e-mails or instant messages. While all my real-life friends were separating themselves from me, I was able to talk to people I had never met about the complicated sorrows of my day-to-day life, from the deteriorating relationship with the guy who was my boyfriend at the time to my concerns about my father. None of them asked anything inappropriate of me. They would talk to me about their relationship problems, they would read my writing and critique it, they would joke with me. Their interest in my life was a comfort.

My junior year had left me feeling devastated, not to mention with a lower GPA and minus one rocky relationship that had at least been something to fall back on, on the worst of days. I had walked out of school on the last day that year in a daze. I went home dreading the next two months of solitude. I sat on my bed and watched movies every day. I spent more hours of the day asleep than awake. I actually looked forward to the ten hours every weekend I spent at my job cleaning out coffeepots and sweeping floors.

For the first two weeks of the summer, I was totally lost in my own little world. I spent hours upon hours every day on The Board, refreshing every few seconds, hoping someone else would be as bored as I was and reply to my posts. By the end of June, I would have been happy to hear from Satan himself if he could have given me an hour of stimulating conversation. I was desperate.

So to say that I actually hesitated for a moment when that instant message popped up on my screen is giving me a lot of credit. If it had been from anyone else, I probably would have typed a response so fast it would have been indecipherable from all the typos. But it was from one person in particular. I knew the screen name—it was the same username he used on The Board. It was a screen name I was so familiar with that I had begun purposely avoiding it over the past few months. My fingertips paused over the keys for a moment while I read and pondered the message.

When I said earlier that I had gotten into the rhythm of The Board with relatively no trouble except for one user, I was talking about this guy. He was sarcastic. He was vindictive. He never wrote in capital letters. He was the gimmicky sort who prided himself on two things: his status as the indisputable King of The Board and his political views, which were so far to the right they would make Ann Coulter blush. We had cultivated a casual loathing of each other, though I was mostly intimidated by him. He hated my political beliefs and tended to make fun of my age. Basically, he took everything I said terribly seriously and enjoyed mocking me way too much. He had insulted me so viciously at one point I was almost certain it made me cry.

So why in the name of all that was holy would he be contacting me directly like this? I was under the impression that he had irrationally hated me since the moment I made my first post. By this time, it had been about a year since I first started posting on The Board. I learned very early on to avoid his topics and posts because he, well, got a little snappy. After an online argument we'd had six months ago, I had ignored his presence on The Board completely. I had two parents and an ex-boyfriend to yell at me—I didn't need the Internet strangers I sought comfort from to yell at me, too.

But earlier that day, I had posted a response to one of his topics, and we'd had what could have been called an amicable exchange. There were a couple of jokes and an actual back-and-forth of ideas, something I did not think he was capable of. It was an occurrence minor enough for me to assume it would never happen again. In all honesty, by then I had wholeheartedly accepted the hierarchy rules of The

Board and begun to admire him for his wit, despite the fact that he was a faceless, nameless person who I would undoubtedly never meet, and despite—or perhaps because of—how often he enraged me. I had always hoped to get in good with him—he was very well liked on the site, almost universally. Maybe then I could get some online popularity to replace my lack of real-life popularity. It might seem irrational, but it made sense to me then and I wanted to find an opportunity for him to look upon me favorably. I didn't think he would look upon me *this* favorably, though.

For some reason, when I think of that first message, I don't focus on how creepy its text was or how I should have run screaming in the other direction (which, in all honesty, is probably what any sane person would have done). I suppose that in hindsight, his personality had become so ordinary to me that his message—one which would have set off a dozen alarm bells in the mind of almost any other sixteen-year-old girl—seemed normal, even flattering to me. I had spent the past year seeking the approval of someone . . . *anyone*, and in my little world this man was as close to a celebrity as I was going to get. So don't think I'm crazy when I say I replied to that message. I had my reasons and, at the time, they made sense.

The message said simply, "yer not 18 yet, are ya?"

It was so blatantly him-like that I was stunned by it. No caps, as per his pattern, and that obnoxiously folksy way of talking that seemed to say, "I may live in New York and spend most of my life on a theater message board, but I'm still a red-blooded conservative middle American just like you." The sexual undertones of the question were practically his trademark.

This guy was known for his inappropriate comments. In fact, on his profile on The Board he had written "lecher" in the space allotted for "Occupation." Nearly every post he made had some sort of innuendo in it; every reply to a female poster included a double entendre. I had gotten used to it, but at the same time it was one of the things I resented most about him. It was common knowledge on The Board that I was only sixteen, as I had put my age out there to prevent sexual advances from being made. So when he asked the question, I was so flustered that I found myself, after a moment's pause, responding, "No, not yet."

I threw up my hands, unsure of what the hell I was doing exactly. And as it turns out, that was the beginning of a very long period of time I would spend wondering what the hell I was doing exactly.

For some reason, I remember minor details about that fateful June day. The sun was pouring in through the window behind me like liquid gold. My father was upstairs, and I was leaning against the wall, cross-legged on my bed, idly watching the TV. I didn't think that day would change the course of my life. Yet somehow he, without my permission or even my awareness, changed everything. Everything since then has been, in some way, the result of that little conversation. For better or for worse, I am who I am today because he found his way into my life. And I know I am not the only girl in the world who has gone through the exact same thing.

Chapter 2

DURING THAT FIRST CONVERSATION, I kept my distance. The whole chat wasn't very long—maybe half an hour—and was mostly about shallow things, like school or The Board. I was suspicious of every word he typed, and I should have been. I waved off his first question as a joke, gave him the benefit of the doubt. After all, we would never talk again, so what was the point, right?

Eventually, he would learn a lot more about me. But at the time, he knew about as much about me as you do now. I suppose that, before I go any further, I should tell you a little about myself.

I was born in November 1990 in the steely gray valley of Pittsburgh, Pennsylvania. My parents were both very young—only nineteen at the time—and unmarried, and their relationship did not last long after my birth, though they tried to hold it together as long as they could for my sake. That being said, they both raised me, very separately but evenly in many ways.

My mother was definitely the tougher of the two on me. Growing up, I spent weekdays with my mother and weekends with my father, so she had me most nights. She went on through college and got her master's degree, eventually going into secondary education. My mother worked her way through school, and she and I lived alone most of my life, so we were incredibly close. She was tough on me, but we were friends at the same time, even through those rough patches all mothers and daughters go through.

My dad, on the other hand, was a different story. On the weekends, I lived with him, which meant that I lived with his entire side of the family. My grandparents, my father, and my two aunts all lived together until my aunts both got married and moved away. So, I spent my Saturdays and Sundays in their three-story house, mostly being with my grandmother while my father worked. I clung to my grandmother when I was young, as she spoiled me and paid the most attention to me. My grandfather was more my teacher. He taught me my ABCs and used to make up stories to tell me. He made me a writer, and in some ways also sparked my interest in politics. Most of his life he worked for a state representative and was very well known in city politics. He would often bring me to work with him. I was a politician by age five. But I wasn't as close with my father, at least not until age eleven when I started emerging as a real person and the distinctions between my parents started to become clear.

I was a kid and, as such, I didn't like discipline—one naturally follows the other. So when my mother took on the role of disciplinarian and my father emerged as the fun, goofy parent, I automatically began to favor my dad. He let me do more and get away with more, and I was a stubborn kid who much preferred that to my mom's approach. I started spending a lot more time around my dad, and even confessed to him that I wished I could spend an extra day or two a week with him. That decision, for me, had nothing to do with which one of them I loved most or who was a better parent. I was a child—my decisions shouldn't have had any bearing on the situation of my parents' custody of me. But, for whatever reason, my father decided to take my confession and run with it, suing my mother for custody. That's when the longest and most painful year of my young life began.

I was twelve years old and I was being tugged between my parents like a wad of chewed gum. My father, who didn't want to protect me nearly as much as he should have, made sure to tell my mother that what he was doing was completely my decision. This drove a wedge between my mother and me that hurts me to think about to this day. She was incredibly angry and hurt and disappointed, and we fought often and quite bitterly. When the case was finally settled with each parent having joint custody, my mother and I managed to repair our relationship. But she and my father were unable to communicate civilly ever again.

When I was thirteen, my father got married. His wife was a woman he had been dating since I was less than a year old and who I had always thought of as part of the family. He proposed to her during the custody battle and promised me we would all be one big happy family together. I was overjoyed on their wedding day. They bought a small house, got a dog, and for a year or so we all lived together in seeming harmony.

But on their second Christmas Eve together, everything changed. I left my dad's house in the early afternoon to have dinner with my mother's family and returned late that evening to find everything different. My dad was home, but his wife wasn't. I figured she had just stayed late at her sister's, where they had eaten dinner. But the next morning when I went to find my dad, their bed was empty. He was curled up asleep on the couch in the basement. Something was wrong.

All morning he was miserable, and all morning it continued to be just the two of us in the house. I enjoyed my Christmas presents and my dad withdrew to his room. Later that day at my grandparents' house, my grandmother and I sat in the kitchen talking before dinner. She asked if my stepmother was coming. I looked behind me to make sure my dad wasn't within earshot before replying, "I don't know. She hasn't been home all day or last night. I think something's wrong."

The look on my grandmother's face told me there was indeed something to be worried about . . . she was too surprised. If it were no big deal, my dad would have said something to her about why my stepmother hadn't showed up yet. Later, I was in the bathroom adjacent to the kitchen when my dad came into the kitchen, and I overheard my grandmother casually ask him about the absence of his wife. He answered gruffly, "She's not coming."

"Why not?" my grandmother asked.

"We're getting a divorce," my dad replied. I could imagine my grandmother's mouth hanging open as his footsteps faded from the room.

He wasn't being melodramatic. A month and a half later he announced their official separation to me. It was the only time I ever saw my father cry.

My dad wasn't himself after that. I spent more time at my mother's, and he spent more time asleep. I didn't know what to do. He withdrew into himself, and I withdrew into the Internet.

During my sophomore year, my two best friends outgrew me. I had a hard time making new friends in the transition between middle school and high school, but they didn't. By tenth grade they started spending time with a larger and apparently much more interesting group of people, and my personality just didn't fit in there. So when they stopped wanting to hang out, I was left alone and had to flounder through lunch periods and walks to the bus stop alone. During my junior year I managed to make some of the best friends I ever had, one of whom was a vivacious and hilarious girl named Lauren.

My dad and I both picked ourselves up a bit during my junior year of high school. He found a new female friend with two kids, one of the girls was my age, and he seemed to like and have more in common with her than me. I was okay with that though. At least he was happy, was doing things again, and was eating well and exercising.

That same year, my mother got engaged to her long-term boyfriend, and I started to feel my life pulling away from the lives of my parents. I was becoming my own person. But at the same time, I was scared and lonely without their security. My senior year was approaching, which meant college and real freedom weren't far away. I missed being a kid and having simple relationships and simple problems. I missed knowing I was loved and headed in the right direction. I missed having someone around to reassure me.

Be careful what you wish for.

Chapter 3

I WAS FLOATING THROUGH THE SUMMER between my junior and senior years of high school. I was in between so many stages that it was impossible to balance. Between high school and college, and therefore between adolescence and adulthood. Between friendships, between relationships, between stages in so many different ways. I was confused, and I was lonely. I was looking forward to my senior year, to eventually finding my own place in a world I was sure just didn't yet understand what I had to offer.

But he seemed to think I had something to say.

Not much about that first online conversation we had sticks in my head except for his surprising interest in me. I probably would have forgotten about it if it weren't for that, would have dismissed him as just another creep. But he was

19

older, and he was smart, and he took time out to recognize what I had to say.

Our exchange stuck in my head for a few days, my mind drifting back to him during the malaise of the following week. But after awhile of not hearing from him again, I put the whole thing in the back of my head and concentrated on scholarship applications and college searches. As June turned to July, my mother and I prepared for a coming vacation and I spent more time lying in bed watching the Food Network and surfing The Board.

Then one afternoon while I was sweating in front of my laptop screen, I heard the soft blip of an IM popping up. It was him again, and I was oddly excited. I glanced at my bedroom door, listening for footsteps on the stairs. I looked out the window to see my mother lying in the backyard reading a book and hurriedly typed a response.

I could've turned back then, and if I had there would be nothing for me to write about today. But I can pinpoint down to the hour when I first got caught up in him. It was during that conversation I discovered enough about him to develop a crush. I learned he was thirty-seven, that he was originally from a town not far from Pittsburgh, and that he was a Steelers fan. I found out he was married, though I didn't press that issue at all. He talked about his favorite movies, his love for scotch, that he was a fan of Ted Nugent. I told him about my family and my college search. We IM'ed for three or four hours that Thursday. He told me about his first love, and the story of how he lost her. I was entranced. There was something about him. He felt important. Charming. And for the entirety of that conversation, he was entirely appropriate. He was a nice guy building a friendship with me, the type of guy who could give me advice when I was having a rough week.

I started thinking about him after that day. A lot.

And I guess he started thinking about me, too, because every time he was online he started talking to me. For the next few weeks, I waited for Thursdays and Fridays—those were the days he was online—and we spent most of those two days online together every week for a month. By late July, I had very discreetly told my best friend about him. And I guess he must have started to see the effect he had on me. Or maybe he was just very drunk. I will never know for sure whether what happened that Thursday before my mother and I left for Colorado was preplanned and intentional or whether it was the result of a lot of vodka. All I know is, in the back of my mind I saw it coming, ever since the day he first spoke to me. But by then, I was willing to ignore my nagging doubts. He probably knew that.

It was late, probably 10:00 or 11:00 PM, when he started getting incoherent. It was common knowledge on The Board that he was a drinker, but I hadn't talked to him drunk yet. It was funny at first; I found myself chuckling at his scrambled sentences and typos while I delivered smart-alecky responses. But then he got a little too close, like a guy at a party who'd had too much to drink and was getting way too handsy. I was beginning to get that uneasy, quiet feeling in the pit of my stomach, the one you get when walking home alone at night and seeing someone walking toward you or hearing a knock at the door when you're home alone. Like you just want to shrink away from the world, just want to completely remove yourself from the situation.

I told him I was going to sign off. I even went to block him, but he apologized for making me uncomfortable. He kept pushing and pushing, saying crude things to me that I refused to respond to, being far too blatantly sexual. I wanted so badly to like him that I let it happen, I let him continue until he needed to say good night, and when he did I dismissed his behavior as the way anyone acts when intoxicated. I had never been drunk, so I went on what I knew. And I let it go. I didn't consider at the time that he was probably priming me, feeling out my limits. Or maybe it was accidental. Who knows? But it certainly set the stage nicely for what happened next.

The next day, my mother and I groggily drove to the airport at 4:00 in the morning to catch a flight to Denver. Eleven days later, when I drove home from that same airport upon our return, I would be a completely different person.

Chapter 4

I HAVEN'T BEEN TO MANY PLACES. I've never been out of the United States, and barely out of the eastern United States at that. But I can say with complete confidence that Colorado is the most beautiful and amazing place on Earth. My mother's best friend who lived in a small town about three hours south of Denver was getting married, and we flew out for the wedding and for a week of gallivanting through the southwestern United States. I was relieved for the break from college applications and work and daytime TV, though I wasn't so enthusiastic about nearly two weeks without Internet access.

But that thought vanished into the late afternoon mist as our rental Jeep pulled away from the Denver airport's vast parking lot and the Rocky Mountains shouldered their way out from a cover of low-hanging clouds in front of us. Pittsburgh is said to be a hilly city. You should never believe that. As we wove through the roads that were sliced out of the Rockies, I realized that Pittsburgh had speed bumps. These were mountains so high that their tops were lost in powdered wigs of rain clouds. They jutted up in woody slopes that seemed to never end. I had gotten two hours of sleep in the last twenty-four hours, but I was transfixed. There was something so quiet about the world around me, like I was being cradled by these mountains. Every thought of the eastern United States vanished. I relaxed into my seat.

We drove to the quiet little ski town of Crested Butte, Colorado. My mom's best friend lived just outside the town, and that's where she was getting married. We arrived a few hours before nightfall, jetlagged from the plane connections, disoriented, and a little nauseous from carsickness and the change in altitude. As we unpacked, I searched for cell phone service and found none, flipped open my laptop to find no wireless networks within reach. I felt a shot of panic in my chest. For me, the reality of ten days without Internet access was like telling an alcoholic they'd be spending ten days with a Puritan family. I was already feeling homesick.

That sentiment faded pretty quickly, though. As soon as we'd settled in, my mom's friend loaded us into her truck for a twilight tour of the town. By the time we reached the hilly ranch where the wedding would take place a week later, the cloudy sky had darkened and the mountains were wearing nothing but a halo of red at the horizon. I fell asleep with my head against the window of the truck, fingertips pressed against the glass. I didn't think much about my life back home after that. At least not for a few days.

After a weekend of camping in the Colorado Rockies, my mother and I set off south in our rental car. We had decided to take a few days to explore and, after some debate about where to go, opted to drive down to the Colorado/New Mexico border to see the ruins at Mesa Verde and then veer west to check out Arches National Park outside of Moab, Utah. After a four-hour drive along mountain passes that corkscrewed over 14,000-foot-tall mountains with two lanes and no guardrails (I think my mother's knuckles are still white to this day), we arrived at a campground outside Mesa Verde National Park where we spent the night sleeping in the back of the rental Jeep. On Tuesday, we explored the ruins, just managing to escape the rain as we climbed back into the Jeep to head to Utah. From the top of the mesa, you could look south and see the golden desert of New Mexico stretching out to the horizon. It started to storm.

Utah was different. It wasn't as mountainous—for the first

time in days we drove down pin-straight highways for hours. But after awhile, the landscape began to change from flat and brown to rocky and pink. Pink rock along the roads, a long pink canyon like a mouth along the left side of the highway. By the time we reached Moab, the world was a russet-colored blur of desert and sun.

Wednesday was spent exploring the massive red rocks of Arches National Park. That night, we found a Days Inn—with wireless Internet access (I felt my heart leaping in my chest)—and settled in for a night of cable TV and a swimming pool. I booted up my laptop for the first time in almost a week.

I was amazed, and a little disappointed in myself, that I had spent so much of the trip thinking about him despite my best efforts not to. He had gotten into my head somehow. I had developed a ridiculous but quite ordinary crush—the kind where you fantasize about your first kiss, about introducing him to your family, about seeing movies together, about those ridiculous relationship-y things. It was a very chaste, pure view of a relationship at the time—I was basically a lovesick teenager trying my best not to fantasize about playing house with a man twenty years my senior. Every song on the radio reminded me of him, and I would randomly wonder what he was doing throughout the day. I would always have that fleeting thought of *I can't wait to talk to him about this later* before I managed to repress it. All of this without even knowing his name, which he had managed to avoid telling me on several different occasions. (Getting my first name out of me was as simple as him asking "wtf is your name, anyway?")

Every now and then when I was lost in a brief spiral of thought about him while we were driving or eating dinner, the part of my brain that still actually worked would pop up and say, "Hold on, wait a second, he's two decades older than you, he lives three hundred miles away, and he's MAR-RIED." I somehow managed to keep that part of my brain quiet most of the time.

It was that nervous pull in my stomach I was trying to repress that night in the hotel as I flipped open my laptop, secretly hoping he would be online. It was Wednesday. He was rarely online on Wednesdays. What did I care anyway? But he was online. And he instantly greeted me. *Like a trained dog running to its owner*, I thought. I grinned a little too giddily.

My mother abandoned the TV in favor of a trip to the pool, and I hurriedly told her I'd come along later, typing furiously. I told him the story of our vacation so far, how beautiful it was here, asked him how things were back there.

He seemed eager to talk, too, as if he'd missed me.

I wish I could pinpoint the catalyst of the profound shift that happened that night, but I can't. It might have been me putting up with his inappropriate comments the previous week, it might have been my funny (and innocent, at least in intent) story about my mother accidentally walking in on me changing, or it could have just been the "we've been talking for a month so it's time to get down to business" threshold, but there was a slow and very obvious increase in inappropriate comments that night.

I resisted his subtle comments at first, like when I was talking about my favorite Billy Joel song, "Only the Good Die Young," and he said that his favorite line was "don't let me wait." But I guess he got sick of my resistance, because he finally came out with this: "So, have you ever had anyone run their tongue up the inside of your thigh in soft, slow circles so that the heat of their breath against your skin rivals the shiver going up your spine?"

I swallowed hard.

To this day I am convinced there was no good response. I have to admit that when I read it, I felt that particular momentary flutter just below my belly button, and a low little gasp spilled from my lips. I knew it would happen eventually, I realized, but I had been hoping against it. And now, there it was, clear as day. His intentions. I had no idea what to say.

So I said something genial and diplomatic. "Don't say stuff like that when my mom's around to see the look on my face." Then I hastily added, "And no, the answer to your question is no."

I could practically hear his evil little chuckle through the computer screen. He asked how often I touched myself. I felt my stomach clench. That feeling was back, the one from the other night, that feeling of discomfort. But it was a little weaker this time, like I could handle it . . . like it was almost okay. I didn't answer. I changed the subject, and he let me steer him back to talking about football. I tried to ignore the nervous flipping in the pit of my stomach. *You shouldn't have been so nice,* I thought. Soon he had to go, and I casually asked when he'd be online next. He responded, "Could be as late as Friday. Why? You wanna prepare first? Candles and music and all that?"

I was taken aback that he had assumed I wanted that. What he was proposing—and I had gained familiarity with it from his passing mentions of doing it with other women in the past—was cybersex. Like phone sex, or text sex, but over the Internet. It seemed to be a favorite pastime of his, from what he'd told me in his overly drunk state the week before. I had tried to convince myself it wasn't what he was looking for with me, but I was wrong. And because I had been a pushover about it up until now, he was assuming it was what I wanted, too.

I wasn't sure what I wanted. I thought about it as we drove back to Crested Butte the next afternoon. He had a reputation, no doubt, and not one he tried to dispute, but I thought he had more sense, or at least more respect. At the same time, if that's what he wanted, it must mean he liked me, right? My mind reverted back to my crush-filled fantasies, and I couldn't help but feel a little giddy that he seemed to want me that badly. Sure, we had only known each other a month, but he took an interest. I fell asleep with Bell Biv DeVoe's "Poison" playing in my head, deciding to let myself see where our relationship—if you could call it that—would go from here.

It didn't take me anywhere that weekend, since I didn't have any other chances to get online. But he was on my mind a lot, and I was stuck wrestling with what all this meant. I tried to convince myself that it was okay, just a friendly thing . . . what was the big deal anyway? He was a catch, and I was lucky. I came home with newfound enthusiasm for what would happen between him and me. That, and a strong desire to someday move to Colorado.

Chapter 5

AFTER A VERY TURBULENT FLIGHT, we returned to Pittsburgh on the first Tuesday of August. On the way home, we'd had a layover in Chicago, and in a half-asleep haze at 2:00 AM, I used the Chicago airport wireless Internet and drafted a private message to him about our travels. Ultimately, I elected not to send it, afraid it would come off as too eager. That was where I stood. I was practically writing notes asking him to check a box to tell me whether he liked me or not. There is no reason a sixteen-year-old girl should feel that way about a thirty-seven-year-old man—a man less than a year older than my father. But there I was, staring at my laptop, waiting anxiously for him to come online.

He didn't that day, or the next, and I returned to my everyday life feeling a little lonely and down, hoping he hadn't forgotten about me. Thursday rolled around and I waited expectantly, pretending to be busy so I could fool the invisible critics around me into thinking I wasn't just waiting for him to come online. And then, finally, he did.

I wanted to type everything at once. He said hey, that he was glad I was back, told me about his new job. I reluctantly said there was a bunch of stuff I'd been dying to tell him and that I'd written him a private message but didn't send it. He seemed to be amazed by this.

"You actually thought of things to tell me?"

I said that I had, not sure whether to be hurt by his surprise or think he was flattered. He didn't mention his inappropriate tangent the previous week, and we started talking about random things like Pittsburgh and pizza and bad 1980s music. He listened to my complaints about the pressures of college applications and scholarships with surprising patience and gave me obvious advice that somehow seemed sage coming from him. I told him about my insecurities, and he pointed out the prom photo I used for my profile picture on The Board, saying, "Why insecure? Yer a pretty girl, if you were legal I'd totally have asked for naked pictures by now."

Despite the implications of what he'd said, the immediate thought that came to my mind was *That's got to be in the top five nicest things a guy has ever said to me.*

We talked for hours until the dreary August day turned to blue twilight and then I was sitting in a dark room with only the TV and computer screen for light. At 9:30 I told him I'd be right back, I had to go say good night to my dad, who always went to bed around that time. When I returned, he perked right up. "So, Dad's in bed, huh?"

"Yeah, upstairs," I said. My room was on the first floor, along with the kitchen and living room.

"So, what're you thinking about doing now?" he asked. There was that feeling in my stomach again. It was pretty weak this time, though—as if something in my mind was saying, "Oh, just go with it."

"Nothing, really," I replied, heart racing just enough to make my face heat up.

"Ya want me to give you something to think about?" he replied.

Whatever happened after that, whatever transition there was, I honestly don't remember. I remember lying in bed afterward, saying good night to him, and thinking wistfully about what had just happened. He had gone on for twenty full minutes, telling me in vivid detail about how he wanted to perform oral sex on me, and I sat there shaking, staring at my screen in delicious anxiety, unsure of what to do with any of it. After it was over, he asked me how I liked it, and I said that he was fantastic. What else could I say? My nerves had evaporated, replaced with a kind of admiration I only had for guys I liked but knew I couldn't have. I lay in bed that night restlessly, going back over how I felt.

Had I liked it? I had to admit that I had. He had said things that were genuinely tender and attentive in a way I wasn't used to hearing. Lots of "gently rubbing" and things like that, nothing severe enough to shock me or scare me away. And if that's all that this was, what was the big deal? It was harmless and sweet to the point of making me grin goofily to myself. I dreamt about him that night, wondering where this would go, what he would mean to me in the future. If only I'd known.

Chapter 6

THE NEXT FEW WEEKS WERE REMARKABLY like the first weeks of a relationship. He was only online four or five times a week, scheduling chat rendezvous with me ahead of time. I bought a copy of *American Beauty* and he started comparing our relationship with the relationship between Lester Burnham, the forty-two-year-old main character of the movie, and Angela Hayes, the seventeen-year-old girl he lusts after. When I told him how much I liked the film, he responded with "Ah, another tale of a middle-aged man and an underage girl." For some reason, I found that to be a perfectly flattering statement.

Ulterior motives didn't start blatantly showing their faces until one night about two weeks into this. My mother was out, so when he got online we started chatting immediately.

We talked about his job—he had been unemployed when we first started talking and had started a new job a few weeks earlier. We got down to what was going on with me. I complained about the process of cleaning my brand-new belly-button ring. This intrigued him, of course. And, for the first time, he didn't tiptoe around it anymore. "Can I see a pic?" he asked.

I chuckled to myself. Just my belly button, nothing else, right? It showed he was interested, invested, not that he was looking to objectify me.

"I don't have a camera," I replied. It was true, actually. The USB cable for my digital camera had recently disappeared in the chaos of the move my mother and I had just gone through. I would have no way to get a picture from the camera to the computer. Deep down I was thankful to have the excuse, but he quickly asked if instead I could take a picture on my phone and send it that way.

So I did. I took off my shirt and snapped a blurry shot of my lower torso, shrugging it off as no big deal. Besides, how could I not seize on the opportunity to ask for his phone number to text the picture to him? That would open up a whole new world of possibilities. So I asked.

"Can't you e-mail it from the phone?" Well, at least I'd tried to get his number.

I was uncomfortable with his notion that it was okay for me to send him pictures of my bare stomach, and I knew this would only lead to more pressure, but somehow I managed to dismiss those fears. It was totally harmless, right? Just the belly-button ring?

I examined the menus in my phone, looking for a way to send pictures over e-mail, finding none on the primitive, basic flip-phone my mother had given me. I was surprised to find myself relieved I wasn't able to send him the picture, but there was still that tug of tension. It was like telling your father you didn't do the dishes after dinner or didn't call your grandmother when he asked you to. It felt like I was disappointing someone whose approval I relied upon.

He was disappointed, sure, but all he really said was that I should find the USB cable for my camera and do it later. I agreed instantly to this delay. Any excuse to keep him happy but keep me from having to do anything I wasn't comfortable with.

Our conversations were longer and more regular now. He usually came online specifically to talk to me, and after a five-day stretch of not finding the time to log onto Instant Messenger at all, he sent me an e-mail asking me if I missed him. He gave me nicknames like "Lex-a-delic" and ended our conversations with "kiss kiss." It was like being in a very secretive and very disconnected relationship.

I only told one person about it—my best friend, Lauren, who seemed somewhat disapproving but glad I was happy and bubbly for a change. When we talked about it, I found myself laughing about little things that he said. At the same time, I avoided telling her everything, like the way he asked for that picture of me and the fact that he was hinting at wanting other pictures. Those were things I kept to myself.

Ever since that night when he asked for the photo of my belly-button ring, he'd been making throwaway comments about wanting more explicit pictures or "art shots" as he jokingly called them. It made me uncomfortable to the point that I seriously told him off about it a few times, and he would always do the Internet equivalent of the affronted shrug and give the "What? It was just a joke!" defense. Maybe he *was* just trying to lighten the mood when I talked about my dad's divorce or giving me a compliment when I was feeling down, but it still rubbed me the wrong way. Something about the requests felt motivated by something deeper.

Chapter 7

I GOT UP ON THE FIRST DAY of my senior year of high school feeling surprisingly good. I put on the casual dress I'd bought a few days earlier and the turquoise ring my mom's best friend had given me in Colorado. All day long, as I talked to classmates I hadn't seen all summer and navigated through my classes, I felt unexpectedly confident. Friends asked me how my summer was and I actually found myself saying "It was fantastic." There were a few times when I had to stop myself from the automatic response of "Eh, it was okay," and remember that I'd actually had a great summer. As I watched the guy I had liked for three years walk down the hall holding hands with his girlfriend and my two ex–best friends sit in class together talking without me, I just reminded myself that I had a secret weapon none of these people knew about. There was a guy out there, a guy much older and wiser than any of them, who thought I was interesting and attractive and smart. It was a great feeling to know that. A surprisingly addictive one.

When I came home that night, he was online, and we talked about school and work for a while. When my dad left to go shopping for a few hours, he managed to slip into innuendo mode. He asked about photos again, and after barraging me with requests for the past three weeks, he was starting to wear me down. I tried to think of a way to do what he wanted. I remembered that I could take the memory card out of my camera and put it into a different camera that I could connect to my computer. So, finally, I gave in.

Checking to make certain there was no one else in the house, I shakily placed my camera on my dresser, setting it to a self-timer. I had changed into a T-shirt and jean shorts upon arriving home, so I took off the T-shirt and stood there, hands on my hips, hoping the camera would only catch me from the shoulders down. I was wrong, of course. It came out as a full-body shot down to my calves, my face turned slightly to the side in a closed-mouth smile, hands on my hips with my stomach totally bare and just the bra covering anything else on my torso. I took a deep breath. Though at first I had been hesitant, there was something strangely empowering about having taken the photograph. It felt different, and sexy, and I hoped he would admire it. I thought I looked good, which was also new. I had doubts about my body, as most teenagers do at some point. I didn't like my hips, or my breasts, or my legs, but looking at that photograph, I was able to find myself a little proud. I sent it to him in an e-mail. He received it almost immediately and was enthralled by it. He told me how hard he was.

I shivered.

Then I erased every record of the photograph's existence. I deleted it from the camera, deleted it on my computer, emptied the recycle bin, and deleted the sent e-mail. But there was that voice in my mind, the one from every *Dateline* story and every warning from my father or my computer-geek exboyfriend. *Nothing on the Internet is ever erased permanently. That'll be there forever, whether you like it or not. But hey, that was your choice. And now he'll have it forever, too. Forever.*

But after he had gotten drunk enough that he needed to go to bed a couple of hours later, I convinced myself it wasn't that bad. I was clothed in the areas where it mattered. I wouldn't be embarrassed if a picture of me from a vacation in a bikini were on an online photo album somewhere. What was the big deal? It would all be fine.

Besides, he liked it. And that's what mattered, right?

That weekend he e-mailed me two photographs. One was of the top half of his body, and I examined it closely. It was a slightly blurry webcam still of a man in his late thirties wearing a white undershirt and black square-framed glasses perched near the middle of his long nose. He had his chin doubled against his chest, eyebrows raised in an attempted come-hither look over the glasses, his visibly blue eyes wide. His hair was sandy and had the pushed-back look of having had fingers run through it many times. His skin was ruddy and shiny, his lips thin with a trail of stubble under his nose. I consciously decided to be impressed.

The other picture was of him from the waist down, completely unclothed. I barely gave it a glance. My heart hammered as I deleted it immediately, sweat forming on my fingertips as I clicked as fast as I could on my laptop's trackpad. I hadn't been prepared for it. And I wasn't okay with it. It was one of those images that couldn't be deleted enough off my computer. It was unsolicited, and if it were ever found I would be unfairly blamed.

Along with the photo, I deleted all of the chats my computer had automatically saved. Suddenly I was paranoid that they would be found. My father had been joking for years that he would be able to see anything I did on the Internet as long as I was using his wireless connection, but I had man-

aged to convince myself he was bluffing since I had never gotten in trouble for anything like this. Still, I thought a lot about
what it would be like to get caught. I didn't like any of the possible scenarios. There was a great possibility that my parents
would be angry enough to try to get him arrested. Them seeking him out and confronting him was even more likely. It was
true that what we were doing was illegal, and I knew that. I told
myself over and over again that I would be devoted enough to
refuse to testify against him, to either my parents or to a court-
room. But I deleted nonetheless, because I wasn't sure how
things would actually go in that situation, and I really didn't
want to find out.

One of the surprising things about that time, looking
back, is how careful I was even from the start. During our
very first conversation I had been paranoid, listening for my
father upstairs or any movement in the hallway. I rarely let
myself talk to him if anyone was even in the next room. If my
mom was downstairs or outside, or my dad was watching the
TV or upstairs asleep, I would still sit on the edge of my bed
listening for creaks and stomps. That must mean I had
always known I was doing something wrong or suspicious,
even if it was innocent at first. Maybe I should have listened
to that instinct from the start. It probably would have made
everything so much easier.

Chapter 8

AS SEPTEMBER WORE ON, we became a little bit disconnected. He was busy with a lot of work meetings and I was busy with school and college applications. I had begun to seriously look at schools now, trying to pare down a final list to apply to.

I had always loved New York City. Since the first time I went there on a school trip in the seventh grade, I had been entranced by the city, by its lights and bustle and arts and food. As a high school student at a school for the arts, I had made friends with theater majors who reintroduced me to the world of Broadway musicals—that was what led me to The Board to begin with. When I was in tenth grade, I swallowed up cast recordings from current and old shows hungrily and had looked for a community online that was just as connected and interested as I was.

I had casually searched out colleges in and around the city, knowing they were difficult to get into and that the chances of my mother letting me go off to New York City by myself were slim. Still, on nights of searching on Collegeboard.com, I would turn on the song "Only in New York" from the cast recording of *Thoroughly Modern Millie* and jot down lists of schools I was interested in around NYC, even before I started talking to him.

With the increasing intimacy—or, at least, seemingly increasing intimacy—of my relationship with him, I began looking more seriously at New York schools. I thought of the possibilities if I lived there. Weekly lunches maybe, or evenings spent in my cluttered dorm room in some twenty-story building in Manhattan. A secret, but real, relationship face-to-face. I was really, really trying hard to ignore the fact that he had a wife who he complained about often and whose mention I avoided like the plague.

I identified a liberal arts college in downtown Manhattan I wanted to apply to, but my mother didn't like that idea at all. She was worried about me being a seventeen-year-old freshman by myself in the biggest city in the country. I am her only child, as she pointed out. So I settled on a small liberal arts college, Sarah Lawrence, just north of the city, which was a perfect place for me since I was planning on at least pursuing a minor in women's studies and Sarah Lawrence is well-known for its exceptional women's studies program. I also decided to apply to five local schools that my mother and I had settled on. But the pressure of the applications and forms and essays, along with scholarships to apply for and schoolwork to be done, was hard on me, especially once contact between me and "him" began dwindling.

For a few weeks, he was only online once or twice, and though we traded e-mails now and then, I was feeling low. One Friday night after a particularly hard week, I ended up eating an entire canister of chocolate-covered espresso beans and staying up 'til 3:00 in the morning cleaning my room and listening to Ani DiFranco. I had heard of seniors losing it during college application time but hadn't realized it would be so difficult.

As a literary arts major at the Pittsburgh High School for the Creative and Performing Arts, I spent every afternoon in creative writing classes, following a different genre every quarter of the school year. First quarter senior year was poetry, and our first assignment of the year was to write a blues-style poem. Sitting in class one afternoon during work time, I doodled quietly in my notebook, daydreaming about what to write.

Over the past few months, he and I had had many discussions about writing. He told me that he was a writer and used to be a poet and was now just a "moderately talented wordsmith," as he so eloquently put it. I had sent him one of my poems when I came back from Colorado over the summer, something I'd jotted down over a long drive through the mountains in the rental Jeep. Considering it was only a rough draft, he'd been pretty critical of it, and I took that as a sign of respect for me as a fellow wordsmith.

For my assignment, I wanted to write something I could proudly send to him, something he would have good things to say about. And I needed to write about something I was depressed about, hence the "blues" part of the poem. So I quickly scribbled "The New York City Blues" at the top of my notebook page and hummed out five stanzas of what I considered to be pretty high-quality writing about my longing for New York, personifying the city and telling it how much I wanted to be there. When I was finished writing, I was pleased with the sentiment. It was a perfect summary of everything I'd been feeling about wanting to move to the city. So I typed it up and handed it in, receiving a perfect grade, something I hadn't accomplished on the first try in a long while.

By that weekend I was feeling lonely and totally ignored. It had been over a week since he'd been on Instant Messenger, though he continued to post on The Board, and by Saturday afternoon I was beginning to panic, imagining that he'd lost interest in me. I wondered why he had no time for me and still plenty for the rest of the Internet. In recent conversations, he'd harped on me to send him more "art shots" and I had ignored his requests quite determinedly. Had he decided I wasn't worth the time and effort if there was no payoff? I decided to find out.

I typed up a private message on The Board and asked for his help. I was working on this poem for class, I said, and I wanted him to take a look and give me criticism since I was having trouble with it. It was just a rough draft, so I was planning on making changes anyway, I wrote. I sent my message off to him, praying for a reply. In reality, the poem I planned to send him was the same one I'd been so proud of only a couple of days earlier, and this was my excuse to send it to him. I was hoping he'd be impressed by the poem and decide that, if nothing else, I was engaging enough to keep around.

He responded with surprising swiftness, a reply appearing in my inbox only five minutes later. Relieved, I smiled to myself, glad to know I wasn't hanging my happiness on something that wasn't actually there. To add to things, he gladly agreed to read my poem and give it a critique—all I had to do was e-mail it to him. So with nerves tingling, I copied and pasted my five well-crafted stanzas and sent them off, waiting impatiently for his response, something that would hopefully read, "Wow, this is pretty good, I don't think there's much you have to change." Or "This is pretty impressive for a sixteen-year-old."

I was wrong.

I got a paragraph of critique back so long there was a scroll bar at the side of the e-mail. He'd picked apart every line to the point where he was regularly writing, "I don't want to rewrite this for you, but. . . ." I felt myself trembling. Maybe I'd been hoping for too much, but I was crushed by the picking dissection of every line of my writing. I told myself that I was a tough girl, that I was mature enough to handle criticism and work from it. I typed an e-mail back to him thanking him and saying I'd work on it. We exchanged a few more private messages over the course of the evening, which was a comfort, and when I went to bed that night, I felt so angry with myself for my bad writing that I couldn't be mad at him for being so harsh.

Two days later, he signed onto Instant Messenger and we had a long talk, a lot of it about his family, about growing up and worrying about his parents getting older. He had been so secretive with his personal life to me, and even on The Board, that it felt special somehow that he would be this intimate. *At least he trusts me enough to talk to me about these things*, I thought. Then he brought up the photos again. This obsession of his was getting exhausting, and I really couldn't keep up the lie that I didn't have a camera since my mother had found the USB cable in a moving box a few days earlier. So I promised him pictures, not really sure what else to do, glad for something to keep him quiet and satisfied.

Over the past month, he had gotten into a routine about cybersex with me, something I was doing my best to warm up to. I suppose at least that had kept him interested. Every time we had a conversation he had some new fantasy he would type up in detail so gruesome and explicit you could never imagine saying such things to another person. But he complimented me intensely each time, telling me how hot I was, how much he wanted me, and, God, did that feel great to hear. So I never denied him. He never asked much from me in these situations, and I went along with an "mmm" here and there, waiting for it to be over and encouraging as much as I could within my own comfort zone. When it was over, I deleted the chat logs.

Looking back, I know I was hinging my entire future on something that wasn't genuine, but it sure felt real at the time. I believed I could have something with him if only I were in

New York. And, yes, I'm aware that picking a school 300 miles away from your family and friends and home because of some older married man you met on the Internet is about as juvenile and ridiculous as you can get. But at that time, he seemed like something good in my life. Something important. I would have done anything to protect that feeling of my heart racing when he said hello to me. I dreamed of meeting him face-to-face all the time—in the car on the way to school in the morning, during classes, before I went to sleep at night. And if college in another state was what it would take, well, that wasn't such a hefty price to pay after all.

Chapter 9

NOT BEING ABLE TO TALK TO HIM as often as I wanted, along with every other thing that was crazy in my life, was starting to take its toll on me. By the beginning of October, I was exhausted and had bad stomachaches and headaches, and for a few weeks my dad let me spend more than one day home from school in pajamas watching DVDs of *Friends* while I waited for my "mental health" to improve. I had a few more incidents like the one with the chocolate-covered espresso beans, though the other times were with mini Baby Ruth bars. I wrote spastically overdramatic poems in the back of my notebook about wanting him to truly see me and want me.

Application deadlines were drawing closer, and my mother and I fought more and more about my grades and the colleges I was applying to. We especially fought about New York. I kept telling her I wanted to go because I loved the city and because Sarah Lawrence was a great school. And while those things were true, they weren't exactly the reasons, and I knew it. My mom still didn't want me going, and it became such a point of tension that we would stop talking from time to time. I was starting to slip.

I began e-mailing him every day or two out of desperation. He had always liked giving advice—I suppose it made him feel like an authority figure—and so I sent him tragic diatribes about how depressed and stressed out I was. He would return my e-mails with punctuality, always offering a kind word or joke when he wasn't giving me long-winded pieces of advice. When those kinds of e-mails ceased to produce the results I wanted, which happened pretty quickly, I appealed to his lecherous side by sending one-line notes that said things like "I had a dream about you last night." Without fail, those notes produced a swift and absolutely enraptured response. And then he started pushing for the pictures again.

I wasn't sure what else to do. I was holding a pretty bad hand, had no ace in my back pocket, and all my chips were already down. I had no magical way to lure him in, because I had finite options when working solely over the Internet. He had become necessary in my life, someone who made me feel reaffirmed when everyone else around me seemed to think I wasn't good enough. So I kept promising and delaying as much as I could but, at the same time, was afraid that the more I did the more he was slipping out of my grasp. And that was unacceptable. So I thought to myself, *What else is there to do? I'll just take the pictures. It's not a big deal, right? Maybe just from the stomach up? That's not so bad. I'll just do that.*

So one Monday night, I sent him two more photographs of me. I took them in the bathroom before I got into the shower, stripping off clothing from the top half of my body and self-consciously taking a picture, totally nude from the waist up. I thought that would be the end of it. He was hooked back in immediately. He started telling me again that I was gorgeous and sexy and incredible and fantastic. I beamed to myself. And then I deleted everything.

But a week later, he wanted more photos, and since the ball was already rolling, I took more and forgot about it. This time they were full body. In return, he wrote me a lengthy e-mail, telling me how amazingly beautiful I was and how honored he was that I'd shared the pictures with him. I felt my cheeks flush as I read his response. *This couldn't be all that bad, right?* It made me feel brave and sexy, and it made him want me and call me beautiful. I looked over the very long list of requests for poses he sent along with his gushing reply and smiled to myself. Nowadays that unfortunate tugging behind my belly button, the one that used to warn me of danger, had been replaced with a pleasant, tingling pang.

He found his way onto Instant Messenger that night—how could he have resisted after I had shown him something so graphic? He had been asking, even begging, for it for months. We talked for a long time, after initial cybersex (which he, of course, couldn't help himself from, because I was so beautiful and sexy and all of that), and I finally got up the courage to ask him if he was doing this with anyone else. As my IM window showed him typing, I felt my heart thumping. I sincerely wished he was going to say that, no, it was just me, but I knew that was naïve. I would have been shocked if it had been only me, though my fingers were still crossed under my keyboard. The first message he sent said, "Just you," and I felt an involuntary grin split open on my lips. *Just me? Wow.*

But then he continued to type.

"A girl from Cali, who's twenty-eight," he continued, and I felt my heart fall into my stomach. "And an old friend who's thirty-six and we only do it every once in a long while."

I swallowed and shrugged, beginning to talk to myself as I typed something back. "Well," I murmured aloud, "you expected there to be other ones so why are you upset? You knew he was that type of guy; don't be an idiot. You wouldn't be enough." I played his answer off like it didn't matter, but I was really shaken by it. Out of that feeling came a new determination. If I couldn't be the only one he casually played with online like this, at least I'd make one hell of an impression. I was going to be the most important one.

I sent him one more photo before I went to bed that night. I woke up the next morning feeling like someone had cursed me in my sleep.

Chapter 10

I HADN'T HAD THE FLU SO BAD in a couple of years. My mom found my forehead warm the next morning when I told her I wasn't feeling well, so she let me stay home for the day. I slept for a few hours in the morning after she left for work, and then went to the computer, finding an e-mail from him responding to the last photo I'd sent the night before. It said simply, "Holy hell."

I wrote back, asking him if that was a good thing, and he replied almost instantaneously that it was. I began to wonder how he managed to have so much time for the Internet at his office. It seemed like he did nothing but e-mail and post on The Board during the workday. That didn't seem like the kind of thing you should get paid for.

I downloaded a lot of music that day, asking him about

song recommendations. He sent me a lengthy list, about a dozen songs, and I downloaded them all. A few of them were okay, but a bunch were thoroughly depressing songs about drinking too much, being lonely, or overdosing on pills. They seemed like angry songs, even for a kid like me who grew up on Eminem and her dad's gangsta rap from the early nineties. Still, some of the music was pretty good. One song in particular stood out to me, a newer-sounding hard-rock track by a band called The Hold Steady. It was much less angry and more fun than the other music he recommended, like songs from bands such as Minor Threat that were a little too intense for my taste. I put the handful of songs he recommended on my iPod and vowed to find a way to like them.

We exchanged about twelve e-mails that day, all friendly and light and very conversational, not at all forced like some of the things I'd had to write to him over the past few weeks. I felt better. The sting of knowing he wasn't as exclusive as I was had worn off considerably. With all the praise he was showering onto me now that I had sent him new photographs, I felt like I had gained some ground. But that feeling didn't last long.

The hardest part about my experiences with him was that it was an addiction. An addiction that was growing considerably worse with each passing day. My mind was even more consumed now than it had been over the summer. I could barely concentrate on schoolwork most nights. Why would I when I could be on The Board trading jokes with him, or talking to him on Instant Messenger, or daydreaming about him? I didn't see much of my friends because I was holed up in my room most of the time. I was sick more often, and my parents noticed that I seemed down a lot, though they mostly dismissed it as the stress of college applications. I wasn't even making as much progress on those as I should have been, especially the one to Sarah Lawrence. All of the essays came out as stagnant and insincere. The truth was I didn't care about most of the schools. And when I tried to write essays for the few schools I actually did want to attend, I never felt like the writing was good enough.

Every night that I didn't talk to him and every day that I didn't hear from him were like a shot in the stomach. I would make myself go a couple of days without writing him in hopes that he would initiate an e-mail conversation, since by now e-mail had become our primary means of communication. He'd told me many times that he was busy, and between work and his wife it was hard for him to find time at night to be online. That was another thing that burned in the pit of my stomach. Every time he said "my wife," I felt a stab of guilt and anger that I had a hard time ignoring. For the first time in my life, I thought about what it would be like to partake in alcohol or drugs and wondered if that would help.

Only a week after I sent him those last three pictures, I couldn't even get a response to a depressed e-mail. One night, I sat half-tearful, refreshing my e-mail inbox for the whole evening with no reply. That was when I realized my relationship with him was becoming a real problem.

Addicts feels okay when they're getting what they need on a regular basis, but withdrawal is a whole different story. He had trained me by this point, and I knew exactly what he wanted in order to keep his attention. His focus might only last for a day or two, but I thought even those few days might very well be worth all the work if I pushed them all together. If it meant doing something I wasn't comfortable with in order to get some regular comfort, I was willing to do it.

So, I waited until my mother left the house one night and took another picture. I sent it to him that night and went to bed, trying to feel good about it, excited at the prospect of hearing from him again. I knew I would. And I did hear back from him, of course, and I had his attention for a few days. I even got an instant-message conversation out of him.

Eventually, this pattern became routine. I would send him a picture or two at night and get a response in the morning. By the end of October, I was taking his requests for different poses and using them. Things went back to how they used to be for a while, and that was a relief. I slowly relaxed back into my life, determined to take care of all the things I needed to get done.

On top of everything else, I committed to participating in National Novel Writing Month in November. It involved writing a 50,000-word novel in the thirty days of November, and it was announced by someone on The Board at the very end of October. I took on the challenge with zeal, already having a topic for my novel. For a good two-thirds of the month, I was obsessed with it, writing 3,000 words religiously every night.

My novel became a story about the journey one girl's life took her on to teach her that love doesn't really exist, a fact I had absolutely convinced myself of over the past few months. Love, especially marriage, was completely useless. Love was something people told themselves they were in when they were lonely and needed someone. And marriage . . . well, I knew of few married couples who hadn't divorced. And of those who were still married, most were usually sad, or lonely, or on the verge of separation anyway. In my own experience, love was the equivalent of infatuation and nothing more. It was typically short-lived, always painful, and pointless for the most part. I was 30,000 words in when my computer crashed and I gave up. It's just as well.

I couldn't tell whether my feelings for him were love or addiction—I had decided there was no distinction to be made.

Chapter II

THE DAY AFTER HALLOWEEN he was online, and the thing I remember most from our conversation was him telling me that he liked my new profile picture on The Board. I had changed it the day before in honor of Halloween—it was a photograph of me in a huge, poofy hand-me-down prom dress I had worn with some cheap costume jewelry and a fake tiara, pretending to be Princess Diana. It was a last-minute thing I had thrown on, but I liked the way it looked so I posted it, hoping to get his attention. I did, although he responded simply, "I looked at it and imagined you weren't wearing any underwear."

Though our e-mail conversations continued to become shorter and more infrequent than they had been over the summer when he was online two or three times a week, we frequently exchanged barbs or private jokes over The Board, which was just delightful to me. He was popular on The Board—he'd been a member for years by then and was one of the original online in-crowd. He had met many members of The Board face-to-face and they, as an inner circle, had a lot of their own private jokes and ways of keeping the newer members feeling left out. I had only been on the site for a year and a half and was far enough outside the circle that I was often ignored by the elite of The Board. It was kind of like high school, except it had less to do with looks and more with who could make the wittiest remark about today's weird news headlines.

He was also one of the very liberal Board's only conservative members, often writing out long, bitter, conspiracy-theory-ridden rants that somehow actually seemed to make sense. He posted more than most members of The Board, which must have been really exhausting since most members seemed to do absolutely nothing else. Despite his political extremism, most of the other members looked up to him because he was something few of the rest of them were—a conservative straight man. He pushed the newer members around like a schoolyard bully, which only made him more revered by the rest of The Board's long-standing members. Basically, if you had his approval, you had the approval of most people on The Board. And, to my excitement, he was starting to pay attention to me there. Which meant that everyone else was starting to pay attention to me, too.

Since I was publicly underage, he knew he couldn't make the kind of explicit sex jokes to me that he made to most of the female members of The Board. For the most part, he took every opportunity he could to make a dirty pun out of something one of the other women said. And that bothered me. I didn't like the fact that he knew I was reading his posts and somehow thought it was okay to crack jokes right in front of my face. It felt like a personal affront. And even if he wasn't doing it intentionally, he was at the very least totally disregarding my feelings. It felt disrespectful, when he knew I was watching, to do the same thing with other people that he did with me one-on-one.

Still, I made my presence on The Board known on a regular basis, always commenting on his topics or responding to him when I could, especially about political things. I have been a political junkie since I was twelve and have spent an average of two hours per night watching MSNBC during the past few years. I planned to go into politics in school, majoring in political science wherever I went. And at the time, the United States was deeply entrenched in the 2008 Democratic and Republican presidential primaries.

Every other day he was talking about some scandal or trip-up by one of the Democrats or posting news stories heralding his chosen candidate on the Republican side, Mike Huckabee.

Now, I will be a die-hard Democrat until the end, but Mike Huckabee didn't look so bad at first from where I was sitting. I started liking him, mostly because my guy online seemed to think he was so great. I even told people in my real everyday life that I didn't think Huckabee would be so bad. It was a testament to how much influence he had over me that he could persuade me that way, but it seemed perfectly okay to me at the time—Huckabee was just a great candidate, right? Still, eventually it became oddly apparent that I was letting myself fall under his sway. I was posting more opinions supporting him than against him, even though I pretty much disagreed with what I was saying. I may as well have been following him around The Board like a sad little puppy. In all honesty, he was so narcissistic that I doubt he even noticed. Or if he did, he definitely didn't acknowledge it.

In the first week of November, I sent him some more photos one morning before school, and after getting the usual response of "ooh" and "ahhh," I decided to go out on a limb. "So I've sent you almost a dozen pictures now," I typed in the body of an e-mail. "Do you think I could at least get your name? Even just a first name?"

His response was only one word long: "Phil."

No last name, but, hey, at least it was something.

By now he'd gotten both my first and last name out of me with little effort, because I figured it was perfectly safe. What was he going to do? I kept telling myself that I was under-age and him saying anything publicly would be doubly as harmful to him as it would to me, therefore it was in both of our interests to keep our mouths shut. It didn't occur to me that he knew my full name, what city I lived in, where I went to school, and what I looked like from top to bottom. And by the time I did finally consider these things, I was into it so deep that no other reaction but trust seemed possible. Hey, he'd proved himself to be discreet—he wasn't posting those photos of me all around the Web—and not totally crazy up until now. Why not keep trusting him?

Chapter 12

IT WAS AROUND THAT TIME when I realized I really didn't know much about Phil . . . at all. Yeah, I knew what he looked like and the general area in which he lived, but 8 million people live in New York City and he never got more specific than that. I knew where he was originally from, a little about his family, that he was married, and now his first name. But in general, I had given him much more of myself than he had given me. I suppose he probably knew when he was saying too much. From what he'd told me, he was pretty much a professional when it came to Internet relationships. He'd been doing this for eight or so years, so he had the whole routine down to an art.

I had never participated in something like this before and didn't even think about things like saying too much, going too far, or getting too attached too quickly. I treated it like a normal relationship. He had started calling me pet names like "sweetie" and "honey" and telling me how pretty I was all the time, and that seemed perfectly relationship-like. Even if I often had to buy those tokens of affection with a photograph or a few seductive comments, it seemed like a fair trade. Half the time I felt as if he really liked me, and those were good days. The other half of the time I felt totally ignored. Those were the days where I spent the evening lying in bed feeling miserable. I had allowed all of my happiness to rely on him.

A few days before my birthday, he let me know he was going out of town on a ten-day business trip. My heart sank. He wouldn't be around for my birthday, which I saw as a true test of how good a friend someone is. Even though he didn't say anything about my birthday before he left, I was hoping that maybe I would hear something from him on the actual day, even if Internet access where he was going was scarce. But November 12 came and went with no word from him. One of my other friends on The Board even posted a birthday topic for me, and ten or twelve people wished me a happy birthday, but he was not among them.

The time away from him wasn't exactly easy. My mother and I fought about my grades, which were slipping, probably mostly because of my depression and preoccupation with Phil. She revoked the reluctant permission she'd given me to apply to Sarah Lawrence, and I was furious. I was seventeen now—I wanted to be able to make my own decisions. In the meantime, I submitted applications to other schools, like the University of Pittsburgh at Johnstown, Chatham University, and Xavier. But, I wasn't completely enthusiastic about any of those schools, so I covertly started applications to American University in Washington, D.C., the University of Colorado at Boulder, and, yes, Sarah Lawrence. If I got accepted, I would find a way to talk to my parents about it then.

My life began to return to its pre-Phil state during his ten-day hiatus and it wasn't all bad. I was definitely feeling down, but I got a lot of schoolwork done and did things I enjoyed, like writing and reading. Still, I thought of him often and checked my e-mail and Instant Messenger constantly to see if there was word from him. But there was nothing—not until November 20 when he returned to The Board. Actually, I didn't even hear from him on that day, and I scoffed indignantly anytime he made a new post without sending me an instant message or an e-mail. I guess he didn't miss me after all.

Then, the next day I was on my way home from school on the bus when an IM popped up on my cell phone. It was

4:00 in the afternoon and I didn't think anything of it, since he certainly wouldn't be home from work yet. Then again, it was the day before Thanksgiving. I checked the message and saw that it was from him, my heart pounding as my finger fumbled to open the message. It said, "miss me?"

I couldn't type fast enough, but I wanted to appear as nonchalant as possible. So I just wrote back, "yes."

He didn't seem to like my lack of enthusiasm. "Wow, I hope you didn't miss me too much, you sound crushed."

So I rolled my eyes and took the time to sarcastically write, "Oh yes, I stayed up nights crying and pining for you." It came out sounding facetious, but it wasn't all that far from the truth.

We IM'ed for a few hours afterward, from my cell phone to my laptop at home and then back to my phone when I had to leave the house. He was surprisingly demanding, asking me for new pictures. He was being absolutely incessant about it. I felt cornered by this, especially since I was around my dad for most of the night and had no opportunity for the discretion I usually preferred when talking to him. I certainly didn't have a spare minute to sneak off and pose for pictures. There was no way for me to pull it off until later that night when I returned home from going out to dinner and found he was no longer online.

So I sent him an e-mail sniping at him for leaving, and he apologized and said he had gotten into an argument with his wife and had to get off the computer. For the first time, I found myself using my tiny source of power in our relationship as leverage, telling him that he wouldn't be getting any photographs if he wasn't planning on coming back online. For some reason, he was able to reply quite forlornly to this through e-mail but couldn't get onto Instant Messenger. I was never clear on why exactly it was so easy for him to e-mail me, even in the evening when he wasn't at work, but at the same time it was so difficult for him to get onto Instant Messenger. He had hinted a few times that there had been prior "incidents" and "troubles" in his marriage due to his IM relationships, but of course he never went into detail. In any case, he kept up a steady conversation with me for an hour or so through e-mail, so once the house was quiet later that night, I set off to take more pictures. It was just the way things worked.

He never did bring up my birthday. Not one time. Not even a passing "Happy birthday, by the way" in an e-mail. I was hurt by it then and am still a little angry about it now.

Chapter 13

MY EX-BOYFRIEND AND I BRIEFLY got back together in late November and had a lovely date the week before Thanksgiving. I was feeling lonely, and so was he, especially since he was off at his freshman year at a school in Rochester, New York, where he knew no one. It seemed logical, or at least practical. I needed to feel like I was doing well at something, even if I wasn't doing well at school or making new friends or even managing my relationship with Phil. In fact, though I tried to convince myself otherwise, I knew I hadn't progressed personally at all since meeting Phil. If anything, I had regressed. I may have felt more confident about my body and how attractive I was, which was a small but important stride for a teenage girl, but Phil wasn't making me a better person. In fact, he was really bringing me down. Meanwhile, Chris, my ex, was and continues to be a great guy and a good friend. Having him around for even a few days improved my outlook on things.

I knew the real reason I was going out with him, though. I was doing it because I was hoping it would inspire some kind of jealousy within Phil, and that he would realize he was protective of me or some sort of trite romantic notion like that. Either that or it would at least show him that I was doing okay and wasn't a total lost cause. *Here, I have a boyfriend . . . I'm not a mess! There are good things in my life that I can't complain about!*

But my reconnecting with Chris quickly devolved into a hollow relationship with nothing but those jealous reasons supporting it. Within a few weeks I was already having doubts about getting back together with Chris and, as had become natural, I went to Phil for advice about it. And per usual, Phil wrote me a very long-winded paragraph of advice, advice which I followed because I believed him. Chris and I broke up in the beginning of December and I was, once again, quite alone with no real prospects. Not that it mattered because, for all intents and purposes, Phil was the only prospect I needed.

Still, it was depressing going to my senior year semi-formal dance alone. I picked out a gorgeous blue satin halter dress and got my hair done and everything, but I was by myself when my mother dropped me off outside the hotel where the dance was held. Though I had a good time, there was still that nagging feeling in the pit of my stomach when I watched groups of friends dancing and laughing together all through the evening. I felt as if I had missed out on something in high school, something I couldn't quite get back. I felt like I was incapable now of enjoying these simple things—things like going out after school to get bagels or ice cream with friends, or even just enjoying gossiping about last night's TV shows or who was dating whom at school. And everything in my real life was absent from my mind 80 percent of the time. Everything in my mind had become about sex and politics and all the things that were important to Phil. I felt a profound rift between me and my classmates that I couldn't cross. Since sixth grade, I had always wanted to be done with school, but for the first time that night I just wanted to feel like a kid.

I arrived home that night to three photos of him in my e-mail box. None were of his face. I deleted them all and went to bed, an empty vortex churning in my abdomen. I didn't want that to be my life.

Still, when I woke up the next morning, I checked my e-mail and The Board. Since it was Friday and the day after the semi-formal, my dad had let me stay home for the morning as long as I got up and went to school for afternoon classes. So I got up around 9:00 and flipped open my laptop and was surprised to receive an IM from him only a few minutes later.

It's nine in the morning on a workday, I thought. *What is he doing online?* He said he had taken each Friday in the month of December off of work since he'd had a few vacation days saved up. I made a note of this in my head, then e-mailed him a few pictures from the semi-formal the night before. We hadn't only been exchanging inappropriate images—I e-mailed him pictures when I got a haircut or of our new puppy, things like that. He pretty much never acknowledged these photos, at least not with the same zeal as the more revealing pictures. He didn't acknowledge my semi-formal photos, either, which didn't really surprise me. The ones that actually mattered usually went ignored.

A few minutes into the conversation he said he was going to try something out. A second later, a request for a video chat popped up and I clicked on it anxiously, nervous about the prospect of actually seeing and talking to him. Sure, he was still 300 miles away, but webcams are good enough nowadays that it feels like you're actually talking to another person face-to-face. My laptop wasn't equipped with a webcam and purchasing one would have tipped my parents off that I was doing something suspicious, but his wife's computer came with one built right in. After a minute or so delay, the chat window expanded to fill half the screen. At first it was dark, and then it snapped to life with the moving image of an average-sized man in a black sweatshirt and glasses in front of an off-white wall. I wondered if he had purposely put the laptop where there would be no defining characteristics of the room for me to see. It wouldn't have surprised me.

He talked into the camera at first but I didn't think there was sound, so I kept typing in the chat window, muttering to myself the whole time about something or other. After a few minutes of speaking much more slowly into the camera, and then giving me the middle finger out of apparent frustration, he very loudly said, "I CAN HEAR YOU." It was then that I realized the video chat included sound, and even though my computer didn't have a camera, it was equipped with a microphone. My laptop's sound was almost completely turned down.

Embarrassed, I quickly turned the sound up as loud as it would go and expanded the video window to fill the whole screen. He looked the same as he had in the photograph he sent me in September, though maybe his hairline had receded just a little over the past few months.

His voice was ordinary for a man in his late thirties, with a lot of pauses for sighs and "uh"s and "ah"s. I found myself

self-conscious about my own speaking patterns, terrified that I sounded too much like a teenage girl. He assured me that I definitely did.

He had, I noticed, a very distinctive habit of glancing from side to side in the middle of talking, as if making sure no one else was around. He was generally fidgety, often leaning back in his chair with his hands behind his head or taking momentary swigs from a bottle of something that looked like juice or Gatorade. Every time his left hand came into view and his wedding ring glinted in the light from his computer screen, my heart sank a little. After a few minutes of talking and settling in, he went in for what I knew the whole purpose of this conversation was.

He stood and, quite suddenly, exposed himself to me. I glanced away from my screen. He couldn't see me anyway, so if I pretended to like it without actually looking, he wouldn't know the difference. He proceeded to touch himself, right there onscreen, right in front of a seventeen-year-old girl who he thought was watching intently. I knew this would happen eventually, I realized. A few days earlier, he had e-mailed me a video that I had deleted but told him I had been unable to open. I imagined it was something very similar to this, and he was making up for lost time now.

After a mercifully short few minutes, he was done, and he

settled back into his seat with a very smug-sounding "So, you liked?" I insisted, quite adamantly, that I had. After all, I had liked the attention. Just not necessarily the form in which it had come.

Besides, now came the opportunity for real conversation. We sat there talking for a good hour and a half. He was much more verbose in person than in text, going on and on about politics and current events. I had to admit I was impressed. At one point, I had to excuse myself to talk to my father, who called while we were in the middle of talking, and when I returned I watched him recoil on the screen. "I turned the sound all the way up so that I could hear you when you left," he said. "So when you came back it pretty much made my eardrums explode."

Was I flattered? Maybe a little.

After awhile, I realized I was going to have to get off the computer and get ready to catch the bus, but he didn't seem to be ready to go. I started wracking my brain for ways to avoid going to school that afternoon, but then he announced that it was time for him to get up and go to the gym, so we said goodbye. He gave a little wave and a coy "Byeeee" before closing out the video. I sat there in silence for a few seconds, marinating in the feeling of what had just happened. I went to school feeling completely fantastic.

Chapter 14

THAT NIGHT I PRAYED HE'D BE ONLINE so we could talk more, but he wasn't. I sent him an e-mail, figuring that wouldn't be too intrusive. He replied to me, and we had a brief back-and-forth that lasted into Saturday morning when he logged onto Instant Messenger and we talked. He had, for the first time, made a few very public and blatant sexual remarks to me on The Board, and I wasn't sure whether to feel delighted or violated. When he suddenly announced he was logging off that morning and didn't come back later like he said he would, I brooded for the rest of the day.

The next afternoon he was online briefly. I waited for him to send me a message, but he didn't, and he signed off again after ten minutes. I was ruffled by this, as it was a rare occurrence, but I decided to ignore it. At least he'd been online, right? Even if he hadn't talked to me, it was a good sign. Maybe he'd be back later.

But he wasn't online later, and he didn't say or do anything toward me for the next few days. I would see his posts on The Board, but I didn't get an e-mail from him or an (IM). For my part, I backed off as much as possible. I had, to this point, been excessively needy. I decided I didn't need to come off that way when things seemed to be going so well. So, I went through the last week of school before Christmas break on my own, catching an occasional nod from him in his posts on The Board, but never getting an e-mail or anything. I changed my profile picture once again to a photograph of me in my semi-formal blue satin dress. To my surprise, I got several private messages from people on The Board complimenting me on the photo. None of them were from him.

I remembered what he had said about taking every Friday in December off, so I begged my dad to let me stay home the last day of school before Christmas break. He didn't, to my great disappointment, but I was able to occasionally check Instant Messenger on my cell phone throughout the day and Phil was never online. Or, at least, if he was, it was when I wasn't checking, and he never sent me a message. It had been a week now since I'd heard from him. It had been months since we'd gone that long without speaking. Naturally, I began to worry I'd done something wrong.

He had said several times that he was going back to Ohio to see his family for Christmas, so I sent him an e-mail that Friday night, a last-ditch effort that I hoped would catch him before he left for the holidays. I got no response, though he found time early the next morning to post a goodbye to everyone on The Board. No e-mail to me personally, though. I didn't know what to think.

Christmas went by in a rush of family and candy and shiny wrapping paper being torn from boxes. I got the first two seasons of *The West Wing* and several seasons of *24* on DVD, and ended up spending a good part of the next week of winter break holed up in my dark room watching them and eating lots of chocolate. I was feeling lonely and exhausted, and the winter days seemed to dissolve from one to the next during the short periods of daylight between dawn and dusk.

Every day I checked The Board for some sign of him, and for days there was none. Then, after a few days he did reappear, flamboyantly announcing his return as usual. He loved broadcasting his life to everyone on The Board, so anytime anything happened to him—even something as simple as a return from a five-day-long hiatus over the holidays—he insisted on letting us all know about it immediately. And so he did, on the evening of the twenty-eighth, reassert his existence, and I waited anxiously for an e-mail or private message or some indication that he was still speaking to me. None came.

I made sure to bump into him on The Board as much as possible, replying to almost every message he posted. He would respond, but there was still no personal contact between the two of us. It had been two weeks now, and I'd come to the conclusion that he was, effectively, totally finished with me. I expressed this sentiment to one of two people in the world who knew that he and I spoke, another friend of mine from The Board. His advice to me was simply to try talking to him again. That was fine, but through my lengthy attempts at trial and error, I had discovered that clinginess did not seem to work well in these situations. Unless, of course, it was accompanied by some sort of sexual advance. And I wasn't sure how willing I was to go there anymore. I was getting tired of that aspect of our relationship.

The next day didn't shed any more light on the situation. I heard nothing from him, nor for most of the day before New Year's Eve. I finally broke down in the middle of the afternoon that Sunday and opened a new private message, typing out a note I tried to make sound as casual as possible.

In essence, I asked him how his holiday was going and said I hadn't heard from him in awhile, just wanted to say hi, and so on. After a moment of sweating over the wording and syntax and whether this was all a crappy idea in the first place, I clicked "Send." It took only six minutes before I got a response, which was surprising, and I was feeling fantastic as I opened up his reply. It was fifteen seconds before that feeling ended.

"Well, besides cutting my finger open and getting a few stitches, I found out I'm going to be a dad."

In middle school we spent a long time in health class learning about the five stages of grief: denial, anger, depression, bargaining, and acceptance. At the time, I was pretty convinced nothing was ever that cut-and-dry, and that no one could predict the order and specifications of emotions someone would feel when grieving. But as I sat there in shock and began to silently mourn whatever relationship I'd had with this man over the past six months, I felt flashes of each of those five feelings. My inner monologue went something like this:

No, no, he's kidding, there's no way that's possible. How could this happen? To him? To me? How could this happen?! And how am I going to get through this? God, what am I going to do? Please, don't let this be true. Let this be a joke. He's got to be joking.

The possibility of him being a father screwed me up in so many ways, I couldn't even begin to comprehend them all. I paced around my room for a few long minutes, this same series of thoughts flying through my head over and over again like flashes of light. I was getting a headache just trying to understand what was happening. Finally, I reached for my phone and flipped it open, dialing the number of the only other person who had any idea what was going on between Phil and me. It rang twice before my best friend Lauren answered.

"I may be having the worst day of my life," I said. And then my cell phone promptly died.

Chapter 15

I'D HAD ABOUT TEN MINUTES TO ABSORB what he had said by then. I read over his message once again, every word imprinting itself onto my brain, and then hit "Reply." I typed a congratulatory message, something as happy sounding as I could muster while still sounding sincere, and sent it. A few minutes later he responded.

"Yeah, I've been meaning to talk to you about that. It looks like I'm going to need to clean up my act a bit, so we're going to have to lay off the dirty talk from now on."

Well, that was that then. That's why he had been avoiding me. It was a bit of a punch to the gut, but oh well. Quitting that aspect of our relationship, at least, was undoubtedly for the best. I went to take a shower and think.

It was under the spray of the hot water where I first felt myself break down.

It was as simple as this. I wasn't only upset because I'd had any dreams of a future with him, though maybe I had been hoping for a short-term future until I could wean myself off of the metaphorical drug. The really traumatizing part of the whole thing was that this man shouldn't be having children, and I knew that. I felt disposable as I had felt for several months, but it hadn't been so solidly confirmed for me until now. I was also surprised by the prospect that he had been close enough, or spent enough time with his wife over the past few months that this could have happened at all. And then, of course, the thought crossed my mind—*What if it isn't his wife he's gotten pregnant?* He didn't exactly specify.

I stayed in the shower for a long time, letting all of these thoughts process as I leaned against the wall and let the sting at the corners of my eyes produce hot, angry tears. I was stupid. I was a dumb kid, and I'd screwed up and gotten attached far beyond what was healthy. I had spent the past few months playing house in my mind with a man who already had a life. I was angry, and I felt immature for the first time in awhile. There was nothing I could do, though. I was unimportant. I was a plaything, useful to him only while he waited for his midlife crisis to resolve itself. A living blow-up doll. I felt so used.

I dried my hair and got dressed, and when my phone had charged enough, I called Lauren again. I kept my voice steady as I told her what had happened, until I got to "He said he's going to be a dad," when I found myself spitting out the words like too-hot coffee. Then the tears came back.

Lauren was silent for a second, finally responding with a sympathetic, "Oh, Jesus. Are you okay, honey?"

I said I wasn't and, in a rush, filled her in on everything I'd been thinking. She told me to come over and we'd talk more. I said I'd be there in twenty minutes.

My mother could tell something was wrong as soon as she saw me. When she asked, all I could say was that I couldn't talk about it and I would be fine as long as she took me to Lauren's. So she did, dutifully, and in the car I did my best to hold back tears. I was unsuccessful.

"Seriously, what's wrong?" my mother asked again, reaching over and brushing a stray strand of hair out of my face.

I sniffled and looked over at her. "Seriously, there are some things I just can't talk about. I'm sorry, but I'll be fine. Just give me a little bit of time and I'll be fine." I wanted so badly to tell her what was wrong, but knew that I couldn't without more serious repercussions. Still, I came so close more than once right then.

She dropped me off in front of Lauren's house, and I rang the doorbell. My friend greeted me with a tight hug.

I spent an hour and a half in her room pacing and spitting out angry sentences over and over again between bouts of crying on her bed. I was angry at him, I was angry at myself, I was angry that anyone had ever encouraged this. I used every swear word I knew, cursing him at the top of my lungs. I snarled out angry laughter, telling myself that he'd be miserable with a kid. How could he binge drink and get stoned on Vicodin with a baby around? No more scotch, no more time to play around with girls on the Internet. He'd be miserable by the end of the first month. And I'd be off at college, perfectly happy without him.

Suddenly I looked up at Lauren. "What if he has a daughter?"

We both sat there and pondered the thought for a second. *What if he* did *have a daughter? Would this man, who apparently had no problem chasing after teenage girls for sexual purposes, even make a passable father to a little girl?* I suddenly felt a whole new heaviness in my head. What was I supposed to do about it, anyway?

After nearly two hours of getting it out, of having Lauren sit there and listen and offer agreement when it was required, we decided to go downstairs and get something to eat. At least the crying was done, though I didn't have any appetite.

When I went home that night, my mom did her best to cheer me up, but to little avail. We watched a movie and I was silent most of the time, lost in the same cycle of thoughts. A couple of times I tried to sneak onto the computer to send a desperate e-mail to the one other friend who knew about the situation, but my mother seemed to sense that the Internet was the source of my trouble and didn't let me. I didn't really want to anyway. At that moment I decided I needed to rebuild my life somehow, and disconnecting myself from all that poisonous stuff was probably the best first step.

The next day was New Year's Eve. After a mostly sleepless night, I crept downstairs to the basement den and wrapped myself up in the throw blanket. Outside, it was sunny, rays of silver making their way through the window above the couch. I was reading a David Sedaris book I got for Christmas, feeling lethargic and empty. It was early, and I kept drifting between reading and thinking and half-sleeping, wondering where, exactly, I was supposed to go from here. I had given over so much of my life to him, and he saw me as unimportant and disposable. To him, I was easily replaced, easily forgotten, and totally devoid of emotion.

For Christmas, my dad had bought me an AirCard and said he would pay for the monthly subscription to its service.

The AirCard would allow me to access the Internet literally anywhere—in the car, sitting at a bus stop, even in the middle of nowhere. A few days before this whole thing happened, my dad had installed it on my laptop and I'd been pretty excited about it. But what was the point now? I sat there and stared at the pages of my book swimming before me. I didn't even want to think about moving to New York anymore.

It was New Year's Eve. I should have been happy and ready to celebrate. But I had nothing to do and I didn't want to think about the next year, either. The future had looked so promising only a few days earlier—all of my college applications were submitted and I was even enrolled in two college classes in the spring to get a jump start on college credits. I had been on my way out of high school. But now I felt like I didn't have anywhere to go when I was done.

My mom and I went to the mall that day, and I couldn't concentrate on anything but the happy-looking couples I saw pushing around baby strollers. That would be his life, an idyllic little world of shopping trips and picture taking and kids' birthday parties. I hated knowing that.

That night, my mom and her fiancé decided to go to a New Year's party, so I hung around the house and waited for them to leave before logging onto the Internet. It was close to midnight when I announced to everyone on The Board that I was going to be taking a break, that I needed to concentrate on other things. I decided it was the healthiest thing to do. If I cut off the problem at the source, there would be no way for it to cause me problems anymore. And I needed to take control of something, to show that I was strong and could handle getting rid of this on my own. I wasn't going to let him, or any part of the Internet, rule my life anymore.

He sent me a message a little after midnight, because he just couldn't leave well enough alone, and asked me why I was leaving. I scoffed, frustrated. Not even ten minutes into the New Year and he was already making me break my resolution. I explained to him that I needed to focus on my life and that the Internet wasn't good for me right now. My answer, though taking a very subtle jab at him, mostly ignored his role in my decision. I just didn't know how to articulate to him how his recent announcement had made me feel. I even understood that how I felt about him, and how much I took our relationship to heart, was ridiculous. Telling him about it would be succumbing to the desperation and adolescent naïveté I had been doing such a good job of not telling him about. Though, of course, I was very plainly showing it to him.

"That's good," he replied in just a few minutes. "That's smart, and so are you. You'll be just fine."

I growled under my breath, fighting back tears again, and replied to him, thanking him and wishing him a happy New Year. I was hoping that would be the end of it, until he sent me a message back telling me to do something rather obscene with an empty champagne bottle.

It took about twenty-four hours for him to break that no sex talk rule, I thought to myself. I shut down the computer for the night and made a round of calls to family and friends, telling them in misleadingly upbeat tones about how great 2008 was going to be. That night, at least, I believed it, and was determined to make it so. That would be the first of many moments of similar determination and renewal in the coming year.

Chapter 16

THAT WONDERFUL RESOLVE TO HAVE A GREAT YEAR lasted about two days. I woke up on New Year's Day feeling melancholy and aimless. I barely ate anything all day. The next morning was dreary and bleak, and I ventured to school in the remnants of white Christmas snow, now gray slush that spilled over the gutters. January 3 was no better, and that afternoon I finally gave in to my self-inflicted melancholy. I typed up an e-mail.

Admittedly, I was manipulative. In the end, I had not really learned anything from the past few months. I still felt the need to use the same techniques to get his attention. On that particular day, I attempted the self-deprecating guilt-trip, telling him that if he didn't want to be friends any longer now that sex was out of the equation, I understood. He replied in typical caretaker mode, "Just because we can't do that anymore doesn't mean I don't still want you to see me as a friend and sounding board for your problems."

That made me feel pretty good. At least, in some slight way, he saw me as more than a body in a photograph. It was reaffirming. I felt like I would be able to move forward more smoothly, even if he didn't still want me in a sexual way. Maybe this would make everything easier.

That first week after getting that e-mail was incredibly productive for me. I bonded with a few people I used to hang out with and learned that I really liked them. Most prominent were Kyle and Charlotte. Kyle was a guy I'd known since tenth grade and had had a crush on the previous year, but when I mustered up the courage and asked him out at the end of junior year, he totally ignored me. As a result, first semester of senior year there had been only silence between the two of us, which I finally broke following the events of late December. Then again, if it weren't for Charlotte, that connection probably would never have happened.

Charlotte was a quiet, sweet, funny girl I'd been close with on and off since the beginning of middle school and whose schedule matched mine during senior year. So we ate lunch together every day and regained the closeness we'd lost over the past few years. Charlotte was Kyle's closest friend and finally managed to get the two of us talking again. The three of us started hanging out and, while watching the results of the 2008 election primaries together in front of my grandmother's TV, I quickly found that we had a lot of fun together. Charlotte and Kyle became a major part of my life after that, and it is the good times with the two of them that stick out as the bright spots during an otherwise terrible few months in early 2008. Because, in the end, no matter how bad that pre-New Year's blow was, the really crappy part was only starting.

As for myself, I picked up a copy of Elizabeth Gilbert's *Eat, Pray, Love* during the first weekend of January and read it avidly. I was hell-bent on growing and improving out of this situation, turning the adversity into something constructive. I was going to be strong and get through it.

Unfortunately, that's not really how addiction works.

Looking back now, it's clear that I wasn't the only one with an addiction in the relationship. Phil grew to need me just as badly as I needed him, something that became abundantly clear on January 8, only ten days after he'd declared there would be no more "sex talk."

I had just tuned my TV to MSNBC and opened my laptop to begin working on a screenplay for my creative writing class when his IM popped up. My heart raced, and everything in me just wanted to close the dialogue box, but I just couldn't. I was bitter. I was probably out to prove something, and I might have been too aggressive about it, because after we talked about the New Hampshire primary happening that day, I pushed the sex subject. I pushed because I knew he would break and I wanted him to. God, I *needed* him to so I could prove to myself that he needed it, too.

He did break, and I was pleased with myself for how quickly it happened. I pushed the tiniest bit and he toppled. Afterward, he kept saying that we couldn't do it anymore, but I knew something had changed. He was relenting to himself, he was rationalizing. "It's okay until the baby comes, then I just have to stop," he said.

I went to bed that night satisfied, because even though I hadn't wanted all the inappropriate behavior in the first place, somehow it felt like I had won. I had, for once, gotten the better of him. At least, that's how it felt at the time. I should have just left well enough alone.

Things sailed along for a few weeks. Gradually, I spent less time with Phil on my mind and more time with my friends, which was nice. I had 'fessed up to Charlotte about Phil, and she was sympathetic, though I don't know that there's any way she could have really understood.

The second semester of my senior year was going to be

an easy one—I wasn't taking anything except for gym and my afternoon writing classes. So I picked up two classes at the local community college and started them the second week of January, two weeks before the end of my school's first semester. Everything seemed to fall into its place. I was doing my best to hold Phil at bay and concentrate on my last real weeks of school work. Still, knowing he would eventually fade away into the abyss of memory was hard to deal with. So one morning, while we were walking to class, I pulled Kyle aside.

"So, I need your help," I said quietly, mounting the stairs as slowly as possible.

"With what?"

"Well, I've decided that I need to get extremely drunk," I said. I attempted to make it sound almost funny, funny enough that he could dismiss it as normal teenage fascination and not anything to do with actual depression.

"I thought that you might be able to help me out there," I added.

Kyle looked at me, amused. "Why do people always assume that I'm the one who can get them alcohol?"

"You're just that type of guy," I said. "See what you can do?"

"Sure."

So that was where I was. It seemed to make sense. Almost every adult I knew solved their major issues with alcohol. Alcohol seemed to make people happy. Maybe it would help me forget, too.

Old habits die hard. By the third week in January, Phil was back to asking me for photographs, but I didn't oblige him this time. My pledge to stay away from The Board stuck for a bit, though not for long. I rationalized that it would be okay on weekends. The school nights that I had to fill with other activities were tough—my room stayed immaculate for a few weeks. I was amazed at how much free time I had now that I wasn't refreshing the same webpage for six hours every night. The realization of just how much the Internet, and the people on it who I didn't even know in person, had taken over my life was alarming. And the fact that I still couldn't completely let Phil go made it that much worse.

Chapter 17

ON THE FOURTH SATURDAY IN JANUARY, while I was out to dinner with Lauren, my mom went into my room to get my dirty laundry. When she saw my digital camera tossed on the floor next to my bed, she turned it on, hoping to see pictures from our trip to Colorado the previous summer. What she found changed both of our lives.

She didn't say anything until Tuesday, after she'd spent three days being distant and emotional and secretly checking sex-offender registries and trying to find me a support group. There were none.

By Tuesday, I had started worrying something was wrong because of the strange way she'd been acting and the fact that my camera was missing. After school that day, I went up to my room to get changed and check The Board, as I usually did, but when my mother noticed me using my laptop she got quiet.

The day before, I had noticed the power cord for my PowerBook had mysteriously "gone missing" and I'd had to charge it at school, mumbling the whole time about my mother being irresponsible. I hadn't realized she'd actually taken it until she stopped me from what I was doing and told me that we needed to talk. And, just like that, I knew what was going on.

For months I had been pondering what would happen if I hadn't been good enough at covering my tracks. I had these weird daydreams of courtrooms and my valiant refusal to give up the identity of the faceless guy who had been doing all of this to me. It wasn't like that in reality. As soon as my mother sat me down and said "I know," I felt myself caving in.

I don't know that the reality of the change my life was about to undergo hit until that night. I felt so many different emotions in that moment that my body immediately began to numb itself from the pain. I was hurt, I was scared, I was horrified. And more than anything, I was ashamed that the thing I was most upset about was the fact that I would undoubtedly be banned from speaking with him ever again. In fact, I would probably be lucky not to be dragged into some criminal trial over the whole thing. As I sat there looking at my mother as steadily as I could, all I could think of when she sat down with a pad and pen in her hand were the words she uttered herself. "I know. It's over."

I was immediately resentful of this, and immediately scared.

I wanted more than anything to just retreat back into my room, back to the Internet, away from all of this sudden and crushing emotional hardship. He was my escape, and he was the thing I was now forced to escape from. It was devastating.

When Mom said it was over, she meant it. Immediately she told me that I was not allowed to go onto the Internet for a long time. She had already contacted a detective from the Pittsburgh police and hadn't decided whether it would be a good idea to press charges or not. I balked at the idea. I felt at the time like I had somehow betrayed Phil by letting this happen, and started to miss him, which I really hated about myself.

It was my fault, after all. Somewhere along the line the photographing and e-mailing had become so routine that I had gotten sloppy and forgotten to delete e-mails and pictures, and that was where my mother found them. From there it wasn't a far leap to figure out what was going on.

I was scared. I knew that I couldn't contact him again— my mother was taking the computer anyway, there would be no more Internet for me—and that thought terrified me. I knew I wouldn't be able to get around such a ban without there being really serious repercussions.

The two of us talked for a long time. I told her the whole story, explaining everything. My mother's sadness toward me quickly shifted to a sharpened and burning hatred for Phil, one that lasts to this day. I spent most of the night crying. We never moved from that basement couch, except for one point when I felt like I was going to vomit and rushed to the bathroom. I didn't want to eat anything, and when she dragged out blankets and lined the basement couch and floor with them so that we could sleep there, I barely slept at all. All I could think about was what had happened the night before, which had been like many, many nights before that.

The night before this fateful Tuesday, I had woken up at 4:00 AM and had not been able to fall back to sleep. My mind was occupied with thoughts of him, dizzying thoughts I tried to repress as I stared at a pulsing patch of pale streetlight on my ceiling. I had thought about how he wanted me, and I wanted him, and how none of that mattered, and it would all be over soon. I didn't know how soon, but it still hurt then. He had wrapped me so tightly around his virtual finger that I couldn't see in front of me. I had no idea what was right anymore. I couldn't deny that I felt a good deal of resentment toward my mother that night, and that I was mourning for the loss of something that had kept me going for the last half year. I immediately missed him. But I knew that from then on talking to him could be dangerous in so many ways.

Both nights were the same. When I finally did drift off to sleep, I dreamed of him. And when I woke up again, everything was dark.

Chapter 18

AS MUCH AS THAT CONFRONTATION with my mother hurt, I look back on it now with an odd sense of fondness. It opened up a whole new time in my life that, at that moment, seemed totally miserable but turned out to be remarkable. That things might turn out okay would have never crossed my mind the next morning when my mother got me out of bed to get dressed and go to school. She promised to pick me up early so we could come back home and talk. The only thing that got me through those first few days of absolute torture was my mother. I was amazed by her strength and tenderness in a situation where I had done something terribly and irreversibly wrong. How had she managed to forgive me so fast?

It was, as she pointed out, not my fault. I had done something really stupid, but it wasn't because I was really stupid or I was a bad person. It was my insecurity and desperation that had been my downfall, and the fact that I happened to run into a guy hell-bent on manipulating a minor. She referred to what had happened to me as a form of sexual abuse, which I could feel myself agreeing with. I tried to think of it as abuse instead of an addiction, because "abuse" made it feel like it was less of my fault. My mother was eager to look at it as his fault because she had read all of the e-mails he'd sent me, and all of the disgusting things he'd said to me. Her vitriol toward Phil was absolutely terrifying.

We haggled for days over whether or not we should pursue it as a legal matter, but after talking to an actual detective, she decided it wouldn't be a very good idea. "First of all," she said as she hung up the phone after her third chat with the detective, "it would be a very long and painful process, and since it's a cross-state matter it would take even longer and be even more of a hassle. Second of all, you could potentially be prosecuted as well because of the photographs you sent and the fact that they could count as child pornography. He said it would be a long shot that would happen, but you still should understand it. And third of all, this guy will get a lawyer to defend him who will try to discredit you and anything you claim happened. It would be a really long and traumatizing thing, and you'd have to tell people that it happened."

We agreed right then and there to not take legal action, but I could tell my mother wasn't satisfied. She wanted revenge so badly she could barely talk about anything else. But still, other things had to be taken care of, and most of them weren't easy. The support group she tried to get me into, which was for general survivors of sexual abuse, turned me away because my particular form of abuse wasn't physical. This made my mother angry, but she did what she usually did in situations like this. She made an appointment with a therapist. I was glad for that, for the most part.

Next came the part I was dreading most. She told me outright that she was going to have to tell my father. The mere thought of my dad finding out made my stomach churn. But she wouldn't back down, and so I told her she could as long as I didn't have to be there. Before she left to see him, I handed her my AirCard. She didn't know what it was, but since he gave it to me, I knew he would want it back now that I wasn't permitted to use the Internet in pretty much any form unsupervised. I gave her my laptop, too, after dutifully deleting any evidence I had neglected to clear away in the first place.

When she came back from seeing my father, she seemed puzzled, telling me that he had taken the news so easily and stoically that she wondered if he didn't already know. "And if he did," she said, "and he didn't do anything about it, that's a whole new issue right there."

I assured her that he hadn't known and that was just the way my dad was. Like me, he avoided problems. No doubt he had probably seen signs, maybe me acting strangely or oddly emotional one day or another, but he couldn't have known and not said anything. He was just good at being in denial, devoid of emotion. And that was fine with me. It made me feel better to know he wasn't furious and demanding an explanation from me. It was a small comfort in the whole mess.

Chapter 19

MY MOTHER TOLD ME HOW PROUD she was of me for giving back the AirCard without being asked. "I didn't know what it was, that thing that looked like a jump drive," she said. "Your dad told me. It shows a lot of maturity that you did that." At least I wasn't completely hopeless.

I didn't talk to my father until the next day. In fact, I didn't really want to talk to anyone. And if there was one person in the world who could understand that, it was my dad. We decided that I'd stay with my mother until Friday. I wasn't ready to deal with anything else.

Thursday and Friday were finals days at school, so I only went in for the morning to take tests and then came home. It was the end of the first semester, and they were the last real tests I would take as a high school student. Friday after my last tests, I sat in the classroom of my high school mentor, Mr. Bishop, for over an hour and tried to find a way to tell him. That was when I realized it wasn't that I didn't want to talk about the situation—I wanted desperately to, to tell someone about it and how I felt. But I just couldn't. Every time I found a way to steer the conversation to a place where I could reasonably spill out everything, I pulled myself back. It was shame, more than anything else. I didn't want people to just see me as "that girl." I didn't want to have those images and those words be the only things people thought of when they looked at me, or the only things that came to mind when they remembered me.

By then, those fears had already come up over and over again in the hours my mother and I had spent talking about everything. How I had wanted to go into politics when I was older, even run for office, but I might as well forget that now. No one would elect someone who'd done what I did, and I would never have control again of whether or not it leaked to the press or came out one way or another.

There was also the feeling that I had rested my entire future on something that wasn't even worth blinking an eye for. When I was applying to college, I was willing to invest every ounce of my reckless, naïve, bipolar happiness on something that didn't even exist. Had I given up my whole future in exchange for a few months of mediocre memories that would be wisps of black smoke in a few years? Maybe now I would never even get to do what I really loved. Maybe I would lose friends over it, or never get to make friends I would have made. Maybe I would lose family over it. It hadn't been worth it. But it was so much easier to see now that I was grounded in reality than when he was taunting me with escapist fantasy. It had been so easy, when reality had so little to offer, to find something that seemed simple and easy and purely happy.

It took me a long time to realize that Phil was willing to take advantage of me—a sixteen-year-old girl who thought she was invincible and that the world was good. He cared so little that, like me, he was willing to throw my future aside for a momentary burst of pleasure. I thought of Phil's own child, the one he'd have soon, and I got even angrier, thinking that he would kill anyone who would do this to a son or daughter of his, and yet it was so easy for him to do it to me. How little he cared about me, how easy I was to throw away after I had given every ounce of my trust and myself over to him. It was infuriating. A whole future, maybe, completely vaporized because it didn't matter to someone else.

As Saturday approached, I dreaded going to my dad's, not because I didn't want to see my father but because I was terrified of the conversation that would have to take place between us. I spent the latter half of Friday at my mother's school, my head down on a desk in her classroom while she graded finals. I just wanted to sleep for a while without any thought, but every time I felt myself getting close, a sudden jolt of reality would hit me and I would sit up again, staring at the blank sheet of notebook paper I'd taken out in case I wanted to write anything down. It was the same thing that had been happening the past few nights. When I actually did fall asleep, all I could dream about was the ridiculous things he'd asked me to do—things I had done and could never take back. My mother saw my depression and did her best to assuage it, even cracking jokes about the whole thing every now and then to try to make me feel better. "You gotta laugh to keep from crying," she'd say.

That afternoon, she decided to pick up my spirits by telling me that I still had my whole life ahead of me. "You're still going to college next year, and that'll open up a whole bunch of possibilities for you," she said.

I looked up from the desk. "I haven't even heard from any of the colleges I applied to. How d'you know I'll even get in?"

She looked thoughtful for a minute and said, "Yeah, that's weird. We applied to Pitt Johnstown in October. We should've heard from them by now. I'll have to give them a call."

While she was on the phone I went to the bathroom, and when I came back she looked at me and said, "Well, I have good news. Pitt Johnstown said that they'd just sent your acceptance letter to the wrong address, but you did get in."

We both burst into laughter at this. For a moment, everything was okay again. I was just a daughter with a proud mother whose kid had gotten into college and it was okay. None of this had ever happened. We relaxed and she hugged me and I forgot. I knew it wouldn't work long term, but avoiding problems and masking them with different emotions, just for a little while, helped enormously.

In the end, I still had to see my dad. I tried to find ways to postpone the visit, but my mother insisted. "You're going to have to go there sometime—you might as well get it over with."

I dreaded having another long confrontation like the one I'd had with my mother. My stomach was churning in that same familiar way as I walked up the steep set of steps to my father's door. I made my way in through the basement and up the stairs, and he greeted me, not with silence or anger or alienation but with happiness. I was stunned. He asked me how finals had gone, what I wanted for dinner, if I'd watched *American Idol* that week. After getting over the initial shock of his normalcy, I gleefully played along, so thankful for his ignoring of the whole situation that I overcompensated, avoiding any topic that might lead to it being brought up, so

I could prolong the peace. I had been talking about it nearly nonstop with my mother for almost four days, and I thanked God for this break from reality—one I might have expected from my father. It was what I felt I needed at that moment.

After saying our hellos, I went into my room to take off my coat and put down my bag, closing the door behind me, and for a moment I collapsed on the bed and cried. Just for a second. I didn't know why. It was partially relief, partially still the fear, and partially missing Phil. Everything around my dad's house seemed to have stayed the same despite every dimension of my perspective changing. My dad's spare laptop, with the Internet capabilities disabled, was still sitting out on the table in the hallway waiting for me to use it to watch DVDs or play games. My room was still the same—the same bed where I'd sat, cross-legged and sweating, talking to Phil over the summer, the same dresser where I'd set my camera with the self-timer on to take those terrible haunting pictures of myself. Everything old was new. I wished everything would just change.

The rest of the night was fine until my dad went to bed and I went back to my room. This was the time of night when I'd usually log onto The Board or look for him on Instant Messenger. But tonight I couldn't find anything I wanted to do. I just sat on my bed for a while, and then I called up my ex-boyfriend, Chris.

Chapter 20

I TOLD CHRIS EVERYTHING THAT NIGHT and Charlotte everything the next. These were people I was praying would forgive me and people I was close enough to that they would need to know sooner or later. And I found that, after those long days of denying it and pushing it down, I needed to talk to someone my age who could hear the whole story the way I was feeling it. There were some things, like the way I was secretly missing Phil, that I couldn't tell my mother. They might not understand and they might not like it, but I kept talking. When I wasn't talking to them, I was staring glassy-eyed at the TV, trying to process the rest of the world I had been shut off from for the past few days.

For all intents and purposes, I felt like I was going through a particularly ugly breakup. There were certain movies I couldn't watch and certain songs I skipped on my iPod. But by Saturday, those songs I had skipped earlier in the week became the songs I turned up the loudest and relished most. They were like snapshots, one thing that would always remain the same and be frozen in time. Music had always meant memories to me. So when the song by The Hold Steady that I had loved in October came on, I turned it up as loud as I could and pressed my earbuds deeper into my ears. I could practically feel the past through the music.

Ultimately, these were my moments of defiance. Yes, I was angry and bitter toward him, but I still missed him. That is the way addiction works. So in those private moments when I was alone with my music or alone in my room, I privately remembered him with fervent fondness. I hadn't loved him, I knew, but he was ingrained in me. I have spent a lot of time over the past two years trying to accept that.

To this day, the only conversation I have had with my father about everything took place that Sunday morning over brunch at a local diner. In the middle of eating and whatever conversation we were having, he looked up from his plate and said, "So, are we ever going to talk about this?"

I was taken aback and nearly choked on my coffee in my effort to look away. "No," I replied simply. It seemed like the right answer. It was the one he was looking for, I knew, and it was the only one I was able to give.

"Okay. Just let me say this, that I'm very disappointed. And that's all—we won't talk about it." He didn't say it angrily; he didn't even raise his eyebrows in the way he always does when he's upset. He just said it, matter-of-factly and even pleasantly, given the situation.

"And just so you know, I haven't told anyone about it. I haven't told your grandmother or your aunts or anyone, and I won't. So, you know, don't worry about that." And with that he shifted the conversation again and went back to his plate of biscuits and sausage gravy. I let the burning in my stomach die down before I took another bite of bacon.

I've almost brought it up about a thousand times since then. There have been scores of fights and dozens of times I've been depressed when I just wanted to blurt out everything and let my dad know it still hurt and that I wished he would understand, but I've never done it. That's not the way it's worked.

In my quiet hours of introspection that weekend and in the weeks following, I thought about the striking similarities between Phil and my father. My father was exactly 353 days younger than Phil, in fact. They were the same height, the same weight, and shared many preferences when it came to music and movies, even expressions they commonly used. I began to wonder whether Phil had grown on me so much because of this, or if it was the kind of thing you were bound to notice about anyone after awhile.

My dad and I have had a hard time communicating fully with each other since then, and I don't know if that has grown organically out of me getting older or if it's because of my relationship with Phil. But no matter how badly I wish I could put everything out there, I still can't stand to tell my father the details of what happened with "that guy in New York." In a lot of ways, I wish my father had gotten angry, had wanted to kill him like my mother did, because I would feel like he cared more. At that moment in the diner, I was grateful for his silence and denial. But if I could go back to that Sunday morning now and answer his question differently, I would in a heartbeat.

I went back to my mother's that afternoon and she knew right away that I had made the wrong decision. When I told her that we had barely talked about it at all she looked at me suspiciously.

"You really think that's the best idea?" she asked, and I nodded. "Well, you're going to have to talk to him about it sooner or later," she said, brushing the hair from my face with one hand.

"Later, then," I said, and went up to my room to crawl under my comforter.

I had the following Monday and Tuesday off for midterm break and spent most of it hibernating. I watched TV and burrowed under my covers. Of course it still sucked, but I took it as a good sign that I could sleep now, even if I was sleeping too much. Depression basically became my state of being. That and boredom. There was little to do besides think when the thing I'd spent 80 percent of my free time doing was taken away so abruptly.

For once, returning to school was a gift. It was something to do all day. Of course, going back to school was also cause for a lot of temptation. There were computers everywhere, in the library and in classrooms, especially in my afternoon writing classes. I managed to avoid the Internet at all costs for a while, telling myself it was for the best. I never checked my e-mail or The Board, and my mother had removed texting and Instant Messenger capabilities from my cell phone so I couldn't contact Phil that way either. My cyberlife came to a complete halt. It was difficult to deal with that for the first week at home and even harder the first week back to school when it was taunting me there, easily accessible with no foreseeable consequences. I've seen a lot of people on the news mocking the concept of Internet addiction or addiction to social networking sites like Facebook or MySpace, but it isn't so funny when it actually happens. And it does. I'm living proof.

Chapter 21

IT TOOK ABOUT A WEEK FOR MY RESOLVE to crack and for me to get comfortable enough in my state of living that I figured it would be okay to check, just once. So I did. I snuck into the library at lunchtime one afternoon and checked my e-mail. I was hoping for just a note, maybe something from Phil asking where I was or if I was okay. When there was nothing, my heart sank. I checked The Board and my private messages there. Nothing. He hadn't so much as wondered where I was enough to drop me a note. That spoke volumes about how he really felt.

So, with that in mind, I dove back into real life more clearly and determined than I had been before. I had been holding on to a trace of hope that he cared and would at least miss me, but now that I knew he didn't, it wasn't so difficult for me to dismiss those last wisps of desperation. I threw a big party for the primary elections that were being held in twenty major states on February 5 and spent the evening having a great time with a dozen or so friends. By now I had told Kyle the truth, and I had even told another friend who I wasn't so close to, but who I thought would at least sympathize. For my election party, my mother bought me a T-shirt that said "I Only Date Democrats" in big red and blue letters across the front. I think she was relieved that I wanted it—her sense of vengeance hadn't quite died down yet.

I got more college acceptance letters at the beginning of February. One for each school to which I had applied—Chatham University, Xavier, Pitt Johnstown, and Juniata College. I had given up on dreams of Sarah Lawrence or any school in New York, though I had privately started on an application to the University of Colorado at Boulder, still holding out hope for going back out West and getting as far away as possible from everything I knew. I never sent that application in. I never even finished it. Probably for the better.

I didn't know which school I wanted to go to. My parents were pushing strongly for Chatham, which is a small, private women's college about fifteen minutes away from both of my parents' houses. Being a teenager, I wanted to get at least a little farther from home than that. But I was accepted at Chatham with a scholarship, so they at least insisted we go and check out the school.

The night after our trip to Chatham, my mother came into my room and settled at the foot of my bed. "I wanted to check in," she said, "and kind of see how you were doing with this whole thing, what you're thinking about and everything."

"I'm fine," I said as cheerfully as I could. I was three or four weeks removed from the implosion, and if there was a significant amount of pain still kicking around below the surface, I had enough to think about that it got covered up. Did I have little breakdowns now and again? Absolutely. I got depressed. I cried. I felt lonely. But I was able to handle all that, better and better all the time. I knew my mom was trying not to think about it too, so I moved the conversation along to colleges as quickly as possible. "I still don't know about Chatham, though," I said.

As far as colleges went, I knew where my father wanted me to go. He was convinced I would choose Pitt Johnstown, but he did not pretend for a second that he didn't prefer Chatham. My mother, on the other hand, did her best to remain ambivalent—I knew she loved Chatham, but she tried to leave the decision to me. She was also partial to Pitt Johnstown since she had gone there. So we did what my mother always did in these situations—we drew out a pros-and-cons list. That list sat on my desk for quite awhile, maybe even months, staring at me with its flashy goldenrod-colored paper, daring me to think about it. I was determined to make my future different than my past had been, though, and the hour and a half of driving time that would be put between me and Pittsburgh if I went to Pitt Johnstown seemed like just the right amount. That night, we dropped the topic after a long, long discussion and I put those thoughts on the back burner. What was important was just getting through the days.

Sometimes I thought about the past. That same night, I went downstairs to write a paper for school on our desktop computer while my mom watched what I was doing from the couch, making sure I wasn't covertly sneaking off to any websites I shouldn't be. I looked for music to play while I worked and found that everything on the computer's iTunes had been wiped out. With a scoff I tried to figure out what to do. I had a short stack of iTunes gift cards sitting on the desk that I had gotten for Christmas and not used yet, so I decided to take a break from working and find some new music. That could only be good, right? Something new and refreshing.

But I couldn't think of anything to look for. I stared at the blinking cursor in the search box of the iTunes Music Store, trying to think of artists I liked. And then one song popped into my head. The one by The Hold Steady. The one that had belonged to Phil, or at least in my mind. So without really thinking about it further, I typed the band's name into the search box. Something new to remind me of something old. I wasn't sure if it was a step forward or a step backward. I clicked on the most popular song, the first one listed on the search results page, and without even previewing it, I bought it. It was a song called "Stuck Between Stations."

Anxious for something refreshing to listen to, I plugged my earbuds into the desktop computer's speakers and played the song immediately. I expected something that would make me feel better, and maybe give me that momentary heart-thumping reminder of Phil the other song by the band always delivered. But this was different. I was immediately pulled in by the song, the slamming guitar, the gut-wrenching keyboard, and the lead singer's familiar bark delivering lyrics that suddenly meant way too much to me.

I don't know what it is about me, but I've always connected emotionally with music. I have almost never cried at a movie, but I cry at songs all the time. I just fall into music in a certain way that makes it incredibly emotional. I've always been told that smell is the sense most connected with memory, but I think for me it's sound. Even right now, when

I listen to "Stuck Between Stations," I feel the same balloon in my chest as I did that first time, a bubble that's filled with adrenaline and sadness and gratitude for something that said so perfectly what I was feeling.

And it was perfect, because I would never have known about that song if it weren't for Phil. I would never have known about that band if it weren't for him. Inside every note of every melody The Hold Steady played, I felt him. And soon that connection helped wean me away from obsession for him into the love of something entirely different—a love for this band's music.

I got lucky, in that as soon as I played a few of the group's songs for Charlotte, she loved them, too. It took only a few days for me to buy every song of theirs that was available on iTunes, which at the time was three albums and a few singles recorded for soundtracks or compilation albums. I burned the albums onto discs and passed them on to Charlotte, and together we loved every song and every lyric and every guitar solo. We talked about them over bus rides to the movie theater or our favorite hangout after school. Unfortunately, we couldn't get Kyle to like the band, but he was always there anyway to groan when we brought them up.

Charlotte, Kyle, and I hung out as much as we got the chance to, and my initial and still somewhat radiating depression had forced me to turn my earlier proposition to Kyle about alcohol into a steady daily nagging. Finally, in the last week of February, I exchanged forty bucks with him in the hallway after lunch and the three of us planned to spend the night at his place Saturday night. I followed Phil's suggestion of vodka. I may have cultivated a healthy bitterness toward him, but if there's one thing I knew he'd be an expert in, it was the right kind of booze for any occasion.

So, on that frigid Saturday night in early March, Charlotte and I knocked on Kyle's front door and dumped several plastic grocery bags filled with cranberry juice and plastic cups onto his bed. The two of us sat down in front of the altar of our collected purchases until Kyle deposited two bottles onto the bed. "Will that be enough?" he chuckled.

Two bottles between the three of us would certainly be enough, I thought. The bottles looked so foreign in front of me, all ice-blue glass and silver lettering. They felt cold enough to freeze water, and when I twisted the cap off of one of them, the smell of hospitals and nail polish remover whooshed out like a genie from a lamp. For a second I was nervous. Then I felt comforted.

Kyle started off by pouring three shots—or, at least, what he estimated to be about the amount of a shot—into the plastic cups and handing one of them to each of us. My two friends swallowed quickly and with no reaction, like taking a quick drink of water, but I hesitated before taking down the gulp and letting out an audible gasp at the burning. For a second it hurt, and then I felt it. The warmth, the spreading of that feeling of hot comfort all through my chest, something unfamiliar and alive and nourishing. It wasn't a memory, it was different. It was totally new.

We mixed the vodka with cranberry juice, and I turned on a few songs by The Hold Steady, to Kyle's whiny protest. After a drink or two, I stood up and almost walked straight into the door with a throaty giggle. I had never been drunk before. For a while, I felt in control of my own future. I felt distracted.

We fell asleep late that night after a series of events that are blurry but mostly uninteresting, and when I woke up the next morning there were tentative rays of sun coming in through the windows.

Chapter 22

I'M SURE EVERYONE REMEMBERS the first time they were drunk. But I remember the morning after more clearly. It was early when the persistent pain in my stomach nudged me from sleep and I slowly reached consciousness. I was still in the tank top and long skirt I'd been wearing the night before, tucked under a blanket between my two friends who were still clad in jeans and hoodies. It had to be around 8:00 AM. Six hours of sleep. I groaned softly. The nausea was getting worse.

Eventually, stumbling to the bathroom became necessary, even if it meant waking the two of them. So I did, falling to my knees on the mat in front of the toilet and sleepily resting my head on the cool toilet seat. I knew that puking was inevitable, and finally I surrendered to it, alternating between blearily dry heaving so deeply into the bowl that I thought it would swallow my head and curling around the base of the toilet like a bear in hibernation.

The sun was breaking through the clouds, casting its bleak, silvery light into the bathroom, a winter sun regaining strength for spring. The bells from the Catholic church down the street where my father had gotten married three and a half years earlier began to chime.

I thought about Catholicism, which led me to thinking about Phil, because he was Catholic and very well might have been at church this very moment. And I would have been, too, if I were a good Catholic girl like so much of my family wanted me to be. I silently confessed my sins to the porcelain bowl I was staring into, damning Phil the whole time. Damning Phil for making me into this in the first place. And then damning myself for assigning my own sins to someone else. And the whole goddamn time, I couldn't get the chorus to a song by The Hold Steady out of my head. All I could hear, in a chorus with the church bells, were the same two lines over and over again. This cycle of feverish thoughts continued for close to two hours until I finally managed to get up and make my way back to Kyle's room where my friends were still asleep. I was shaking and my arms and neck were covered in cold sweat, but I felt cleansed.

Not just physically, but emotionally, too. In all honesty, I hadn't counted too heavily on drinking to actually help my depression, and it hadn't. It was getting the alcohol out of my system that had done it. Getting the poison out.

That afternoon, I wrote something that could very loosely be called a poem, just a long string of thoughts with no periods or punctuation, just thoughts directed at Phil that kept streaming out of my pen for two and a half pages of notebook paper. By the time I finished writing, the sun was pouring in with real warmth, and I felt powerful again.

Chapter 23

I WISH I COULD SAY THAT I never felt depressed again after that, that I never got lonely or missed Phil again. That's not the case, though time spent with Kyle and Charlotte and my mother's support were helpful in making it better. My therapist helped, too—she was young and had a sense of humor and completely understood where I was coming from. But that still didn't prevent me from thinking about him, though more distantly and bitterly. And as much as it hurt, I did still long for his attention.

I fell into a few days of real depression in April when I was reading Phil's blog. Despite not having my own computer anymore, there were times when I broke down and used school computers or my friends' laptops to check e-mail or The Board or even his blog, though I restrained myself as much as possible. I had come to a place where I settled for knowing him on the periphery, not talking directly to him, but sneaking glances at his posts on The Board or the blog I had never read when we were talking. And then one gloomy Friday in April, he posted an update about his wife's sonogram. He was having a girl.

Reading about his unborn child was not exactly life affirming. Actually, it was infuriating. This man who had talked to me while I was sixteen years old in a way that few men would even dare to talk to an adult prostitute was, in less than six months' time, going to have a female child to raise. I wanted to scream at someone. This man, who had asked me to call him "Daddy" in a sexual context more than once, was having a daughter handed to him. I was angry at God. I wondered if there was a God. Because, really, what kind of God would allow that to happen? I was quiet for the rest of the day, ignoring even my father's pressing to tell him what was wrong. I didn't even know what to say.

Other hits came in the form of rejection by the new guy I tried so desperately to make like me to replace Phil. He was a funny guy in his mid-twenties from my Introduction to Political Science class at the community college, and he was a nice distraction for a bit until he started wanting exactly what Phil had wanted from me—sex, and not much else. I never did sleep with him, thank goodness, but he got me to wondering about a few things.

I began to question whether all men were like Phil and this other guy. I knew the saying from TV shows and YA novels and Lauryn Hill songs that guys are only about "that thing," but I had never really believed it. Had my very first boyfriend been interested in physical stuff? Sure, but he'd almost preferred long talks over coffee to making out, and I had been hopeful that all guys would strike that balance.

My latest relationship and its subsequent crumbling led me to my second new uncertainty. Would anyone ever want me for anything else again? Did I not seem to have anything else to offer but my body? Was I worth anything more? When we were talking or doing whatever it was that we were doing, Phil had given me such a self-esteem boost, but now in retrospect it was the opposite. I didn't feel empowered by my sexuality anymore. I began to mourn it. Even resent it. I had always considered myself an intelligent, interesting, strong-willed young woman, but now a whole half of the human species was telling me otherwise. Guys were either ignoring me or using me for my body. And I had just gone along with it. After the new guy called it quits by basically ceasing to return my phone calls, I did give up. Not just on him—on every man. And that was okay for a while.

Giving up on men was probably a positive step, considering I had chosen to attend the all-women's Chatham University. After a lot of debate with my family and friends, I decided that I had so many more options at Chatham than I did at other schools. Plus, maybe staying close to home would be the best thing. Sometimes staying safe can be good at first. We managed to compromise, and I decided that I would at least live on campus so that I could be independent but still close. Yet, even after I signed all the paperwork, I could still feel the tug of Sarah Lawrence and all the faraway schools that were so different than what I had here. I told myself that after a year or two I would transfer somewhere else, that being stuck here was just a temporary state of being.

READER/CUSTOMER CARE SURVEY

We care about your opinions! Please take a moment to fill out our online Reader Survey at **http://survey.hcibooks.com.** As a **"THANK YOU"** you will receive a **VALUABLE INSTANT COUPON** towards future book purchases as well as a **SPECIAL GIFT** available only online! Or, you may mail this card back to us.

First Name		MI.	Last Name

Address			

State	Zip	Email	City

1. Gender
□ Female □ Male

2. Age
□ 8 or younger
□ 9-12 □ 13-16
□ 17-20 □ 21-30
□ 31+

3. Did you receive this book as a gift?
□ Yes □ No

4. Annual Household Income
□ under $25,000
□ $25,000 - $34,999
□ $35,000 - $49,999
□ $50,000 - $74,999
□ over $75,000

5. What are the ages of the children living in your house?
□ 0 - 14 □ 15+

6. Marital Status
□ Single
□ Married
□ Divorced
□ Widowed

Comments
_____
_____
_____
_____
_____

BUSINESS REPLY MAIL
FIRST-CLASS MAIL PERMIT NO 45 DEERFIELD BEACH, FL

POSTAGE WILL BE PAID BY ADDRESSEE

Health Communications, Inc.
3201 SW 15th Street
Deerfield Beach FL 33442-9875

Chapter 24

WHEN JUNE ROLLED AROUND, to my never-ending amazement, I graduated high school. The following summer was quiet and dull, punctuated by occasional nights spent in Kyle's room with various kinds of liquor and many, many songs by The Hold Steady. All seemed to be just fine until August, when I began to feel the slow, creeping effects of my chronic fear of change beginning. A major life shift, such as going away to college and being an adult, can bring up turmoil so deep and massive it has the potential to put you in therapy all on its own. But I was still dealing with the underlying and constantly nagging feeling of Phil meandering through my dreams and the ups and downs of my daily emotions. He was still hurting me, like poison that never quite works its way out of the system. And by August, the birth of his daughter was approaching and I was nearing a time when I would be able to freely use the Internet again. The thoughts of dealing with a whole new life that I wasn't quite prepared to handle, along with the thoughts of an old life I still couldn't deal with, were suddenly met with feelings so crushing that the Friday before move-in at Chatham I found myself bursting into tears in the middle of a restaurant over lunch with my mother.

I actually can't remember what triggered the breakdown, but it started a domino effect that changed everything. I cried for a while, feeling so angry and hurt and furious at him for having put me in a state where I just couldn't let him go. My mother took a deep breath and got that protective look that told me she was thinking about all of the creative and exotic ways she could make his life miserable. Then she got sympathetic again. "Lex, this isn't the kind of thing you get over right away," she said. "I mean, I expected it to take this long. Probably longer. I'm not trying to say that I don't have any faith in you. You just don't become okay with these kinds of things overnight."

I nodded. I knew that already. It had been really hard at first, and then it had started to get a little easier, but now it was like February again all at once. Why couldn't it at least get all the way to a slow underlying burn and then work the hurt out from there? I could handle that. But these outbursts were not okay.

"I mean, when this happened to me I went through the same thing," my mother said. She had revealed to me upon finding out about Phil that she had, at a much younger age, gone through a similar kind of abuse and it was part of the reason she'd been so upset about Phil in the first place. She was always vague about it, and I was okay with that, as I wanted to know as little as possible. But her commiseration now was invaluable. I wiped my cheeks with a paper napkin and listened. "I was angry for such a long time, and finally I decided I was going to be done with it. So I sat down and wrote a letter, and I told him in the letter about all of the pain. I just sat there in my room for a whole day and did it. Maybe you should try that. Even if he never reads it. And he can, if you want—I guess I could find a way to get it to him if that's what you really wanted—but just writing it for yourself, I think that could make you feel so much better. Putting everything on paper."

That sounded like a good idea to me, but at the same time, I felt like I needed him to read it. After the initial rush of emotions, I knew what it was that was bothering me—it was that ticking time bomb of a due date that was approaching. I knew his daughter hadn't been born yet, because the apocalypse hadn't happened, and also because there had been no trace of news on his blog or The Board. But it had to be soon. And I actually felt guilty. Guilty and angry and still hurt, but mostly guilty. Overwhelmingly so.

I had participated in sexual acts with him, even if they were just over the Internet, while I knew his wife was pregnant. I had kept to myself what he had done to me knowing his wife was pregnant with a girl. I had continued to keep it quiet. Not only had I not told his wife—I hadn't told the police. I had willingly let this happen without giving anyone else but him the opportunity for full knowledge of the situation. I felt terrible for his daughter. I felt that if anything ever happened to her I would be partially responsible. I hadn't done anything when it mattered. The guilt itched at me constantly. And, truth be told, I felt guilty, in some small part, for still wanting him and for knowing that this was probably my last opportunity. These last few days before he became a father were the last chance I would have to get his attention and I still wanted that, or at least the tiny, pushed-away voice in my head still did.

Chapter 25

I DECIDED TO GO OUT ON A LIMB to soothe that aching once and for all. I did something stupid, I'm not going to lie. But I refused to let him make me feel guilty, or hurt, or angry, anymore. So I wrote him an e-mail.

I told him that I was still around, that I'd missed him, and that we needed to talk about something. I guess he had missed me pretty badly, too, because he was on Instant Messenger that night and sent me a message right away. I had gotten Instant Messenger back on my phone, but hadn't used it very much because I didn't want to risk anything. But at that moment, it came in handy.

Yes, it was a thrilling feeling. Yes, I was happy to hear from him again. I wasn't so angry that it blocked the old feelings that immediately came flooding back, and after an exchange of pleasantries, when he finally asked me what we needed to talk about so badly, I almost didn't say anything. As crazy as that is, and as many months as I had spent building up resentment and fury toward him, he melted me. All I wanted was to bask in his positive attention a little longer until this had to end again. I would have bent backward for him at that moment if it meant a little more praise or conversation. So much for the healing process and the idea that distance and time would make everything better. All that bitterness and anger meant nothing now. I hated myself a little more every time I told him I didn't want to talk about anything specific.

Finally I came out with it. Slowly, and surprisingly shyly, I expressed to him my concern. "Well, you're going to be a dad soon, and I'm just kind of concerned about some of the stuff you used to say to me."

I was surprised he was even listening to this, let alone responding to it. "Alexis," he said, "I understand why you're worried, but I'm not going to let my daughter be like you. I'm going to make myself available for her to talk to me about anything, unlike your parents, and she's not going to have the problems you did. Besides, she's not going to see the Internet until she's twenty-five."

That stung. That was possibly the coldest, most biting

thing he could have said then, and I felt a prickling in my chest like I'd been shot with an arrow. *Who the hell did he think he was? Blaming me? Blaming me for what he did?* I was seething, sweating a little as I stared at the tiny pixelated screen of my cell phone. *I was the one with issues who made this whole thing happen?* I was so hurt. This one person who had pretended to understand me for months, who had helped me solve so many of my "problems," was able to dismiss me as some fucked-up kid who was nothing like the ideal child he was going to have?

But, of course, I didn't say any of that. I just accepted his response on IM and shook privately, internalized what he'd written to me. I told him I wished him luck and that he'd better make his daughter a Steelers fan. What was I going to do? As much as I hated him for saying it, I honestly believed that everything he said was absolutely true. I did have problems, obviously. I had oodles of problems that I was continuing to perpetuate on my own just fine. There I was, talking to my biggest problem of my own free will, not being nearly as cruel as I should have been after all those months of picturing how biting I would be to him if ever we talked again. How could I blame him for saying what he was saying when it was clearly the truth?

After that, I did write the letter. I spent the next evening in my room alone for hours, and I typed out an angry, bitter diatribe that, in the end, was more than five pages long. I cried into my keyboard, I slammed my pillow into the wall over and over again. And it worked. In fact, it worked way too well. It worked so well that I got out all my anger, leaving just enough room for the longing for him again. And I'd already opened the door. The sadness and the wanting again still there without the fury, so why not keep going back?

The week that I moved into college was a week of regression. I spent long periods of time with both my parents, clinging to them. But I also spent a lot of time on my phone. And on e-mail. And I settled back into my groove with him. I even got him to admit in passing that he had missed me and wondered where I was, though it took my prompting for him to bring it up. He got me back into conversation relatively easily, since we had a lot to catch up on and I was so desperate for any contact with him. When I finally moved into my dorm, I continued this for a week or two, and then the thing I prayed never would become a reality did, at last.

The morning that I found out his daughter had been born, I called up Lauren. She was at school over an hour away and didn't have too much time to talk, but I spoke to her in a flat voice for ten minutes or so about the situation, just in complete disbelief about the whole thing. He had a daughter. I didn't want to live. He got to have a family, he got to be happy, and I got to be lonely. How did he win? It hadn't hit me until his daughter was officially born that he turned out to be the lucky one.

"Well, that's not true," Lauren said. "You've got your whole life ahead of you and now he's stuck in his."

That wasn't easy to hear at the time because it felt like such a cop out, but she was right. I knew that a week later when he was making sexual advances at me while holding the baby girl. Yes, eventually, I would be all right. But he never would be.

He and I talked on and off until mid-October when it stopped again. His e-mails hadn't really made a difference— I had spurned his advances and fatherhood was starting to catch up with him, so they were mostly just friendly anyway. I would have let it go completely if I wasn't still lonely. I hadn't really made new friends at college, mostly because I was so hell-bent on spending every free second with my old ones that I didn't have time to see anyone else.

Through September, October, and most of November, I spent a lot of nights sleeping on Kyle's couch. He, Charlotte, and I were inseparable. She hadn't made a lot of new friends at college either, and Kyle hadn't gone on to school at all, so his days were filled with work and not much else. We all needed a safe haven during a difficult transition. But maybe if we'd tried a little harder, we would have been a little better off. Eventually, communication between Phil and me halted when I made myself stop e-mailing him or trying to talk to him, and though that was difficult I thought with determination that it was all for the best.

I discovered this the first time I actually did try to get out of my comfort zone and move from the Internet—where I still spent 80 percent of my free time in those first few months—into the real world. Near the end of November, a girl I knew from my work-study job was playing acoustic guitar at a club near school and performing some songs she wrote, so I grudgingly made myself go. Not that I didn't want to, but I was nervous around people I didn't know and honestly just wanted to go back to my room and surf the Web until I went to sleep. It was a Sunday, and I had spent the entire day online feeling miserable and doing my best to resist sending Phil an e-mail. I went to the show that night feeling melancholy and uncomfortable. I left the show feeling better than I ever had before.

I don't want the impression here to be that I needed a man to make me better, or even that I just needed a man in general. That isn't the case. I had managed to disconnect myself from Phil pretty much on my own, though quite miserably, and if what happened that night hadn't happened, I might have been able to continue that. I think the most important thing that occurred that snowy Sunday night wasn't so much that I met a guy—it was that I met a friend.

His name was Colin and he'd started an awkward conversation as we were both standing around without anyone else to talk to. That conversation lasted three hours and eventually led to a kiss, an exchange of phone numbers, and a whispered "You're so beautiful" as he nudged my cheek with his nose. I hadn't heard anyone say that in a very long time. In fact, not since Phil told me so while praising the photographs I sent him. But I wasn't thinking about him that night.

The day of Colin's and my first real date Phil meandered back into my life through an e-mail written as if we'd never stopped talking. I smiled to myself as I read it. Thank God I didn't feel the nagging need to reply that had plagued me for the past year and a half. I closed my laptop.

Epilogue

THAT WAS MORE THAN A YEAR AGO, and it feels like an eternity now. I'm not going to pretend that I was done with Phil after that, or that I was completely okay. It still hurts to this day. Not so much missing him—hell, I know he's still waiting for me and I could go back to him anytime I want to—but regretting him, and feeling like I have to answer to myself for what I did with him. I'm not so much trying to get past him as past myself.

I knew I was going to have to tell Colin about him, and I did a few weeks after we started dating, spilling out everything in one breath and then holding it, waiting for him to look at me differently or pull away from me. But he didn't. He hugged me and told me that he loved me, and that he was so sorry. Around Colin, I don't need to feel insecure or desperate. He doesn't think about my body as much as the other things that make me who I am. And the things about me that everyone else didn't like still seemed beautiful to him.

That wasn't the last appearance of Phil in my life. I don't even know if his last appearance has occurred yet. I'm sure it hasn't. I have learned over the years that as much as he might shrug to himself and say that I was just a fun little plaything he decided to seduce one night, he needs me just as badly as I needed him. He turns up every now and again, and we might even be cordial and have a nice conversation or two, but I put my foot down a long time ago and he has not made a sexual advance toward me since. I always come to my senses eventually and disappear on him—it never takes much time.

The important thing, I think, is that emotionally I don't feel the need to have him anymore. I have gone weeks, even months, without so much as thinking about him or uttering his name to anyone. These may seem like small victories, yes, but it's getting better and better all the time. In a way, I think we will probably always be intertwined in each other's lives, for better or for worse. I still haven't met him in person, and it's been a very, very long time since he's seen any photograph of me, let alone an inappropriate one, but we keep tabs on each other. I wouldn't invite him to my wedding or put him on my Christmas card list, but I will always be aware of his existence. Partially to protect anyone else that he might do this to, partially to satisfy my own morbid curiosity. My mother still hates him, and she has been joined in this fiery and undying hatred by Colin, who is a pacifist but probably would've bought a bus ticket to New York carrying an ice pick in his backpack by now if I hadn't stopped him. It's nice to know they care.

It might seem weird for me to be able to deal with my past so lightly now, but the truth is, it's mostly a preventive measure, to prevent this from happening to me again, whether it be through him or someone else, and to prevent him from doing it again to another innocent girl. That was the main reason I considered trying to get him convicted of this crime two years ago. I know there was another girl before me—he's talked about her—and who knows? There could be more to come, though apparently he has taken to the role of doting father quite well.

I still worry about that sometimes, but hopefully his daughter really was a blessing. Maybe she has grounded him and made him realize that he did a terrible thing to me. He has, more than once, finally accepted responsibility for my pain and my problems, and that was a comfort. But I believe he is, and will undoubtedly always be, a sociopath, so who knows how long those tendencies will stay beneath the surface?

The scary thing is there are thousands and thousands of men out there who do this every day to thousands and thousands of young men and women. My story isn't necessarily just about me—it's also about all of them. I will never forget when my mother got off the phone with the detective back when she first discovered my secret and told me that there were thousands of cases just like mine in the Pittsburgh area alone.

How many people have watched shows like NBC's *To Catch a Predator* and thought that those girls were so naïve, that it would never happen to them? I did. I thought I was too smart for this to happen to me, too. But it's not about being smart or naïve. It's about being manipulated. The truth is that I got really lucky. There are kids—both boys and girls—who have died because of the same thing I went through. The fact that Phil lives hundreds of miles away seemed like a curse back then, but it was really a blessing. Who knows what would have happened if he'd lived close enough for me to meet him in person? Or if he had been aggressive enough to close that distance gap between us?

As for me . . . well, I'm not completely okay, but I'm happy now. Somewhere along the line, I started realizing that I am an amazing person who deserves better. I've forced myself out of my comfort zone enough to make some friends on campus, but I do still see my old high school friends all the time. I don't look in the mirror and see a sad, worthless body to be used anymore. I see a person. I don't just see skin or breasts and hips and thighs. I see a face. And now I know that other people see that, too. It was there all along—I just let someone else draw attention to other places. I don't think that will happen again.

I'm still with Colin, and we're still about as overjoyed to be around each other as we were the first week we met. I still spend nights at Kyle's house sometimes, though not nearly as often, and with much less alcohol involved. And I see The Hold Steady every time they come within a hundred miles of Pittsburgh. No doubt I'll continue to until they split up. I do owe Phil thanks for introducing me to them, though I no longer connect him with the band. There are too many positive memories of their music that have replaced the negative ones.

Even though I do regret the worst aspects of my relationship with Phil, I can't deny that he helped me in some ways. He made me a stronger person and helped me to see great things in myself that I had never known were there. By getting over what he did to me, I was able to see my strengths and positive qualities. For that, I am grateful.

I'm not angry anymore. I think that's the most important thing. I was angry for such a long, long time that I couldn't let it go. Angry and hurt. But once I started feeling okay, even indifferent, about everything . . . that's when I knew I was getting past it. Nothing he can say can send me flying headfirst into a breakdown the way it used to, nor can memories of what he did to me. I'm better than that. I've got a whole life ahead of me. He might have taken a tiny bit of my past, but my future is mine.

Book Club

Discussion and Questions for ALEXIS

1. In her book, Alexis writes about the way television shows like *Dateline* portray online solicitation. Do you think the issue of teens being solicited by online predators gets enough attention in the news? Too much attention?

2. How aware are your parents of the kinds of things you look at and do while you're online? Would you consider it a violation of your privacy if your parents tracked your online communication? Why or why not?

3. In *Alexis*, the thing the author has feared the most—being discovered by one of her parents—happens. Yet ultimately, it was this revelation that enabled Alexis to begin the painful process of closing the door on her harmful

relationship and move on. Have you ever kept a secret from your parents or a close friend only to be relieved when the truth finally comes out? What happened?

4. Alexis's mom tried to find a support group to help her daughter cope with the fallout from what happened to her, but was unable to identify a group that would accept her because her abuse was cybersexual, not physical. What do you think the emotional, psychological, and physical differences are between these two kinds of abuse?

5. Do you think online predators like Phil should be arrested and prosecuted for their crimes? What do you think of the child pornography laws that prosecute teenagers for emailing sexual photographs or sexting?

6. How prevalent do you think sexting and other risky online behavior is among teens today? Do you consider this to be a serious problem? Mostly harmless? What is the reasoning behind your point of view?

7. Alexis shares her story of being lured into a cybersexual relationship with candidness, bravery, and honesty. Do you think her story could have a positive impact on another teen who might be stuck in the same sort of situation?

8. Do you think Alexis' experience has forever changed her life? And if so, for the better or for the worse? What do you think Alexis might have learned about herself through her experience?

About the Author

ALEXIS SINGER attended the Pittsburgh High School for the Creative and Performing Arts as a writer and is currently a sophomore at Chatham University in Pittsburgh, PA studying political science and women's studies. She is nineteen years old.

More Louder Than Words Stories

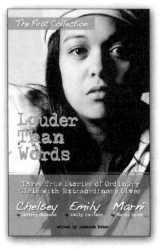